HOW TO BE A GAMES USER RESEARCHER

RUN BETTER PLAYTESTS, REVEAL USABILITY AND UX ISSUES, AND MAKE VIDEOGAMES BETTER

STEVE BROMLEY

Cover design: Chloe True
Editor: Samuel Heaton

How To Be A Games User Researcher/Steve Bromley —1st ed.

gamesuserresearch.com

Dedicated to all the fallen SkiFree players, who weren't told that pressing F allowed them to outrun the monster.

CONTENTS

FOREWORD

Video games are an exceptional creative medium. They matter to everyday people: as an outlet for creativity, for exploration, for competition, or for simple respite from the drudgery of daily life.

Great video games are brought to life by the everyday hard graft of real people; through creativity, compromise, humility and collaboration of diverse developers. Game development teams bring together technicians, artists, designers and operations, all in the name of creating magic together from nothing.

And when their inspiration is forged into art and code, their imaginary worlds must meet our real one: a world full of everyday players who are busy and forgetful, disparate in skill and knowledge, surrounded by hundreds of new games, and hungry for novelty.

Games user research is an essential voice for bridging this gap: between the product of unbridled creative imagination, and the product that an everyday public will enjoy.

Being a games user researcher is a fascinating and rewarding career path. You'll find the day-to-day routine of the role to be meaningful, but also find joy in the privilege of bringing meaning and clarity to the work of others. You'll be empowering passionate creatives of many disciplines to do the best work of their lives. And, in turn, will drive forward the whole development of remarkable experiences to be enjoyed all over the world.

With this remit comes daunting responsibility, and games user researchers are expected to develop a broad set of soft and hard skills. From the researchers' core competencies of behavioural observation and data analysis; through interpersonal and persuasion skills; to hard, technical skills like video editing, statistics, and information technology. All within the context of the highly-secretive and yet very public world of professional video game development.

Steve Bromley's book is an exceptional catalogue of professional advice, purpose-built to develop your skills in this domain. Every page is filled with Steve's hard-won lessons and examples from the day-to-day realities of game development. I certainly recognise my own experiences in its guidance, in both my career-defining successes, and in my failures. I wish I had had this resource in my early career, as you do now.

Every professional domain undergoes change, and game development is no exception. Ever-easier access to game development tools, hardware and know-how means an evermore crowded, competitive landscape for new video games. These changes place greater importance on ensuring games are building toward exceptional quality during development. Game development always seems to be in times of change. At the time of this book's publication, we're on the cusp of a new console hardware generation, and seeing new business models, new genres and new technologies shift the landscape of interactive media, all while still reeling from the mass adoption of smartphones, and the creative potential of virtual reality.

Game development is defined by change. It's a domain driven by curiosity and a desire to push technology to tell new stories and find new fun. As a researcher at the heart of development, you will be the one to change the game.

Our toolkit of games user research processes have withstood the test of time for more than 40 years. Through the future adoption of new technologies, continued maturation of our discipline and all the unforeseeable changes that our future will inevitably bring, I have no doubt games user research will be here in another 40. Helping game developers seek the stories they've yet to tell, the players they've yet to please, and the fun they've yet to find.

Sebastian Long
Director Of Player Research

INTRODUCTION: MAKING GAMES BETTER

Games user researchers help make games better. This has never been more important for the industry than it is now.

Both during my time at PlayStation, and on games projects since, I have continued to be impressed by the impact that even small user research studies can have - both by revealing significant usability issues which risk derailing the game, and uncovering new creative opportunities inspired by player behaviour. This book aims to teach you how to be a games user researcher and be able to do the same.

Games user researchers make games better in two ways. The first is by helping the people who make design decisions, such as artists, designers and producers, understand their players better. This will help teams anticipate the impact of design decisions, and increase the chances of them creating the experience they want to make.

The second and more common way in which user researchers make games better is by putting real players in front of early versions of the game to check that players are experiencing them the way the creators intended. This allows changes to be made before launch so that players have the best experience possible.

User research reveals problems

Game developers can easily forget how different they are to actual players. This is not only because developers are often highly experienced gamers, but also because they have played their own game before. This means they already understand how it works, what they are meant to do, and where they are meant to go. They also assume players read tutorials, unaware that no-one has read a tutorial without spamming the 'skip' button since 1978

Not running user research studies means that problems may not be discovered before launch. Once the game is released, it can become painfully obvious that some aspects aren't understood, or not experienced in the intended way. Big games with expensive marketing campaigns only get one go at a first impression, and a poor experience leads to confused players and poor reviews. This will ruin the game's launch and risk the failure of the game or even the studio. Later in the book, we will consider why issues like this occur, and how they can be avoided.

Some studios do casual playtesting already - putting players in front of their games inside the development studio, or at trade shows, to see if they like it, or if they get stuck. That's a good start, but lacks the rigour or depth that a trained researcher brings. Players in these environments are biased in ways which prevent the findings being as 'true' as they should be. Much like a DIYer can put up a shelf, but not build a house, anyone can run a playtest, but a games user researcher will do a better job at finding trustworthy and reliable information to inform design decisions. The value of running games user research studies lies in finding true, actionable results that extend beyond obvious issues.

A user researcher should therefore help teams recognise the difference in reliability between rigorous research studies and casual playtests, which can be hard for untrained observers to spot. Poor-quality playtests create risks. There is usually a difference between what players say and what players do, and many biases make it difficult for people to accurately predict their future behaviour. Professional user researchers work hard to minimise bias, select appropriate methods, and ensure that the results from their studies are reliable enough to make important decisions with.

This book will help

Overall this book hopes to introduce the role of a games user researcher and help the reader apply the skills to their own role - whether they are a student looking to start a new career, a user researcher hoping to start working in games, or someone already working in games looking to inform their decisions with better information from players.

The first part of the book looks at the game development process and dispels some myths about how games get made. It aims to be an introduction for someone who hasn't worked in the industry before.

The second and most substantial part of the book is guidance on how to run games user research studies to uncover useful information and inform game development.

The final section explores some topics around getting a job and developing a career as a games user researcher.

Since it is a reasonably new field, much of the language around user research hasn't settled down, and people use different words to describe the same concepts.

In this book, some of the terms we'll use include:

- *User Experience (UX)* will be used in this book to refer to the broadest definition - the experience that a player has when playing the game. This is created by the combination of everything - the gameplay, the difficulty, the graphics, the usability, the perceived value, the controls, etc.

- *User Research* is used to describe running studies with users to inform game development. In this book this is synonymous with UX Research.

- *A study* describes a single cycle of coming up with research objectives, defining the correct method to answer the questions, running and analysing the study, and debriefing the findings.

- *Playtest* is a difficult term. Some use it as a synonym for study. Others use it to describe a specific type of study or to describe a less formal method of getting feedback from players than a study. In this book, it is used as a synonym for a study.

There is also a glossary at the back of the book, which will help if any of the terms used are unfamiliar. Words from the glossary are **bolded** when first used.

As we will cover, games user research doesn't intend to redesign a game - it aims only to reduce the gap between what a **designer** wants to make, and what they are actually making.

Games offer fantastic opportunities to have new, creative and emotional experiences - and this is all too often held back by the gap between the creator and the player. Together we will help studios reduce that gap and make games better.

WHY IS GAMES USER RESEARCH NECESSARY?

As we will see, making games is difficult. Making successful games is even harder. Unlike other software, no-one is forced to play games, and players will quickly move on if it is confusing or dull.

The people who make games are different to other players. They have spent years thinking about and playing the game they are making. This can make it impossible for developers to anticipate what the experience will be like for a new player - real players may not act in the expected way, and will not understand what the designer hoped they would. This isn't because players are any less smart than developers, just that their history with the game is different.

Because players, not developers, are the ones who buy games, we need to make sure players understand them. Games need to be usable before they can be fun.

Once these **usability** issues are discovered, it can be tempting to fix them with obvious solutions. Adding tutorials, text or additional UI elements seem easy and can be the first fix a team tries. Unfortunately, these solutions are often ineffective - without understanding real player behaviour, the timing, presentation or contents of these solutions won't work for players.

For more complicated issues, we need confidence that the issues are really resolved for players. Running iterative user research studies to discover whether issues are fixed can help us move beyond ineffective solutions and find more elegant fixes. Every problem is solvable, and it's easier to find the right solution by observing and understanding player behaviour.

Games user research therefore identifies problems throughout development, giving designers the chance to fix them before it's too late. This ensures designers create the game that they want to make, and creates better experiences for players. Better games de-risk financial investment, and lead to strong studios that survive in a competitive market.

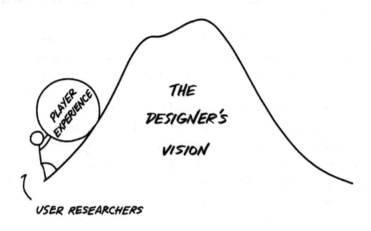

User researchers help raise the player experience

Better games, happy players and successful studios all sound pretty important to me. Let's get started!

PART 1

HOW GAMES GET MADE

Being an effective games user researcher requires understanding how games are made. Knowing how the development process works, and who does what, will help identify the right time to run studies on each aspect of the game. It also makes it easier to direct research **findings** to the right people - greatly increasing the chance for them to be acted upon.

Understanding games development is also important for building trust in the quality of a researcher's work. When running research studies, part of the job will be sharing the findings with developers. Being able to talk credibly about games development will help increase trust in a researcher's competence - making it less likely the findings will be dismissed, and increasing the impact of research studies.

This section of the book discusses some aspects of games development, to give a primer to the industry for people new to it, including:

- Why working in games is great

- Some common myths about what games development is like

- The games development process

- The roles within games development

- What are some challenges that games developers face?

At the end of this section, a new researcher will know enough about the process of games development to be comfortable talking about the process with other professionals.

WHY WORKING IN GAMES IS GREAT

Working in video games is great for many reasons. Firstly, as an entertainment medium, games put joy into the world, and their existence is an ethically positive thing (...mostly). This can be inspiring - a nice change from the tech dystopia we live in where many digital jobs involve working on ways to spy on people and sell their personal data.

Secondly, games are seen as a prestigious industry to work in, and the type of job kids want to do when they grow up. To outsiders, working in games sounds like non-stop fun and there's the opportunity to work on brands that people have heard of. Unlike working in insurance, it's a 'cool' place to work (especially because people assume that every studio makes blockbuster **'AAA'** games).

Working in games also represents the cutting edge of technology, which can be interesting. Often the first commercial application of new technology is in games - **Augmented Reality** games have been around for well over a decade, **Virtual Reality** games for longer. Games have always been at the forefront of bringing cutting edge technology to the public, such as with motion sensing controllers. Because games are often looking for a technical novelty, the problems researchers are faced with are often new, and are interesting to investigate and solve.

Working in games also means being credited. Having your name recorded forever as a significant contributor to the development of a game or experience can be very rewarding and I always made a point of keeping a record of my own credits. Again this is different to other types of software - websites don't usually have credits (perhaps because people want to avoid being blamed for the tech dystopia previously mentioned).

So, working in games must be great, right? It involves being recognised as working on interesting problems in an industry people are excited about.

Well, yes - but there are some downsides too. Before looking deeper into how games get made, and the roles involved, we'll first address some misconceptions about what making games is like. These are not the only challenges with building a career as a games user researcher, but we'll save those for the end of the book!

BUSTING MYTHS ABOUT WORKING IN GAMES

There are some assumptions that people have about how games are made. Addressing these before committing to a career will help avoid disappointment!

It's not sitting around playing games all day

The first myth is that working in games involves sitting around playing games all day. Unfortunately, that's mostly untrue - just like people working in a car factory don't drive Ferraris all day. Instead working with project management tools such as JIRA or editing Excel spreadsheets is much more likely to be a typical development activity, just like any software development job.

There are a couple of exceptions, which involve more game playing. The first is roles like Quality Assurance (QA) who play to look for bugs - this also isn't the same as playing the game for fun. Instead of experiencing it as a player, their role is to comprehensively search for bits that are broken, which is a different challenge altogether. Imagine running into every wall in *Grand Theft Auto* looking for buildings where the camera goes through a solid wall - the task takes weeks and is not fun at all.

User researchers will play through the game they are working on to be familiar with it, and be able to recognise issues. Unfortunately, playing will not take up the majority of their time.

Perhaps the closest that working in games comes to this dream of playing games all day is the friendships it creates. Everyone who works in games is likely there because of their shared interest in gaming, and so socialising can often be based around playing games - but usually not as part of the workday.

It's not just coming up with cool ideas

No-one's stopping you coming up with new ideas, but it's unlikely that they will get made. Unfortunately 'coming up with ideas for games' isn't a real job, at least by itself. In many large studios, the idea is imposed by someone in charge of the studio, a creative director, or shadowy figures with money, and so 'what type of game should we make' is often a decision that is in place before a team is engaged to make it.

Even if this wasn't the case, coming up with the idea for a game is easy, and many people could do it - it's not a full-time job. Instead, it's the implementation of that idea that is more challenging, and where game designers focus most of their time - deciding how a combination of features and scenarios will combine into a coherent experience that delivers the promise of the game. Much of this is extremely complicated, detail orientated, iterative and requires close collaboration with a wide team - not just sitting down and coming up with ideas.

The exception to this may be working within indie games, where an individual, or a small team, comes up with an idea and creates it. This usually requires the person coming up with the idea to also have some applicable skills that help create the experience. An indie developer is unlikely to have the money to pay a large team to build it, and without payment, no professional team will be interested in making a game idea they didn't come up with.

When actually working on a game, making design decisions is often a collaborative effort, led by designers. However, games user research is primarily a role about evaluating design decisions, rather than coming up with them. If your perfect role is to decide how parts of games should work, consider a career in design.

It's not easy

If you believe online comments, making games is easy and developers must be stupid because it's obvious what they are doing wrong. Despite the confidence of strangers on the internet, this isn't the case.

Making games is subject to a lot of constraints, most importantly; time. Games sold in shops make no money until they are complete, and cost money all the time staff are employed. There is a very real deadline on how long they can be worked on before running out of cash. This means priorities have to be decided, and **features** often have to be cut to ensure the game is delivered on schedule. This is particularly important for big franchises, where advertising space is purchased well in advance of launch, and the cost of delaying can be extremely expensive. Even on free to play games, deadlines created by funding or publisher deadlines create time pressure.

On a much smaller scale, any design decision requires balancing trade-offs and a deep understanding of the impact of the decisions. Making a small change to how one ability works can have huge ramifications throughout the game. User research studies can help inform these decisions, but these trade-offs are not easy to anticipate or prioritise. It is beyond the capability of most people complaining on the internet to correctly anticipate the impact of their suggestions.

When people say mean things online about developers, they fail to understand the context in which those decisions have been made and the factors that informed those decisions. In real life, this can be a very difficult job for designers, and is a skill that needs to be practised and informed by real data from studies. It is not an easy task.

It's not all *Call Of Duty*

A lot of games get made. In 2019, over 8000 games were released on Steam alone. Of those, less than 20 would be household names that everyone will recognise. The odds are that you won't always work on a big, famous title like *Fortnite* or *FIFA*.

There are opportunities to work on high profile titles since it is often larger studios that will have the budget or the opportunity to run user research studies. However, there is also a lot of competition to work in games, and roles with big studios are in demand. While it is possible to work on the most famous games and franchises, it will often require effort and compromises to achieve. This is explored further in the last section of this book.

Working on smaller titles isn't necessarily a bad thing though. I found some of the most receptive teams for user research were the smaller games - something built by a team of five often had the creative freedom and autonomy to be able to react to research findings in a more meaningful way than on titles built by studios of over 300 people. Being able to have a recognisable impact on the games being worked on is extremely rewarding, and small teams can often be the best ones to work with.

Understanding all of the above points before starting on a career in games will lead to realistic expectations and help someone make an informed decision about starting a career in the games industry. Working in games is a job, just like any other, and there will be days when it doesn't feel worth it. Despite this, it's a job in a cool industry, working with a lot of passionate people, and can be enormously rewarding if entered into with a realistic understanding of what it is and how it will work.

GAMES IS A BUSINESS

Although games are a creative art form, making games is a business, and ultimately funded by someone who is hoping to make enough money to continue doing it.

The commercial success of games ensures that the studio can afford to make more games, and avoid closing down. This is particularly risky for many studios with multi-year development cycles. The company needs to be making enough money from launches to sustain the leaner times during development - which can incentivise studios to make safer choices, such as sequels, rather than trying something novel.

This also has an impact on people's jobs security. Games suffer massively from boom and bust times - there are points in the development cycle where large teams are required, and points where less work needs to be done. To avoid expensive people sitting idle, or being fired because there is not enough work to do, many studios work on multiple titles at the same time. This allows them to stagger the development times so that while one game calms down, another ramps up and the team size can be kept consistent.

So, to avoid job losses and run a sustainable studio, games need to be successful. Luckily user research can help with this. User research studies can help make a higher-quality experiences, by ensuring that players understand what they are meant to do, are able to do it, and that people enjoy the experience - increasing the chance that the game is a success. The methods for doing this are explored in more detail in the second part of this book.

Although commercial success is important to make games development sustainable, it doesn't mean that it's the only motive for creating games - they are an artistic medium and many people are passionate about creating them because they can be interesting, creative and fun.

When working as a games user researcher, the majority of opportunities to influence games will be on larger titles, which can afford to employ a dedicated user researcher or hire a research agency. Indie developers often lack the budget to have a user research specialist on staff and will rely on feedback gathered from more informal, less rigorous studies than a dedicated user researcher would run. This has some risks, as will be covered later in the book.

As a user researcher, understanding the business behind games and how your game makes money will help prioritise **research objectives** and ensure that studies tackle the most important problems developers have.

HOW VIDEO GAMES GET MADE

There is no single correct way to make games. The development process varies a lot based on the size of the team and maturity of the processes they choose to follow. Because of this, it can be difficult to define a single process and say 'this is how games get made'.

The process can be messier in practice than the theory suggests. Conflicting demands on people's time, and a hard deadline, will disrupt the design and development process, and the stages can mash together. This is particularly evident with the trend towards '**games as a service**' (GaaS) which promises continual content updates, and selling early access. These both move the launch earlier, before the game is complete.

At a high level, some of the steps that a game will go through during development include:

- Before green light: Coming up with an idea for a game, and convincing someone to fund it

- Pre-production: Exploring and building the core of the game

- Production: Scaling up the game, then refining it

- Launching the game

- Making post-launch changes and updates

We'll go through each of these in turn, and look at how these might be relevant to someone working as a games user researcher.

Before Green Light: Defining the concept

Games are expensive to make and require a team to be paid for years before the studio finishes a product that can be sold. This usually means that someone has to be asked for money to fund development, and they will want to know what they are going to be getting in exchange for their money. Green light meetings are where these decisions take place.

During this stage, the idea of the game is defined and described, in a way that will help others understand what it is trying to achieve. This can be a written document but is often supplemented with other material, like videos made by cutting up clips from movies, films, and other games, to convey the feel of the game. It can also include a prototype demonstrating some of the **mechanics**, and market research information such as reports on the size or value of the potential number of players in a genre.

A playable prototype helped Media Molecule communicate the concept behind what became *LittleBigPlanet*.[1]

A successful idea for a game will be informed from lots of different sources. Some sources are commercial, such as market research done to work out what topics or genres might sell well, or what **intellectual property** (IP) is available to use, or which other games have been

---

[1] VIDSerbius (2007) *Little Big Planet Prototype*. Available at: https://www.youtube.com/watch?v=HQLDNmllbiU (Accessed: 12 June 2020).

successful recently. Other inspirations are artistic, such as what would be a fun and interesting idea for a game.

For user researchers, there are some studies that can help development at this stage, and other studies that feel like they would be useful but are risky and care needs to be taken. We will review a few of each.

The game's concept can describe the idea of the game, some of the core mechanics, characters, levels, and how it is different from other games. The concept is often used to explain the idea of a game to professionals, such as people who can finance it, or people who need to understand the vision to work on it. One potential topic for research studies would be ensuring that people have understood the concept correctly. This would require the researcher to understand what the idea is, and what the designer wants to convey to their current audience. They would then show the concept to other professionals, and explore their understanding to ensure it matches the designer's intent. This can help inform changes to how the concept is presented or explained to make sure that it correctly articulates the vision.

Some game ideas will also require a better understanding of a player's knowledge and the space that they plan in. Developing motion-based games, VR or augmented reality games will require players to have an appropriate space to play in, and may involve some novel interaction methods. Understanding player's contexts, where they play, and what they already know will help inform design decisions, particularly for new mediums such as VR. Similarly, understanding how and where people play mobile games will help inform decisions about features. For example, learning that most people play without sound would help decide whether to make game mechanics that rely on sound.

A tempting but dangerous **study** is getting players to talk about how much they love the concept. As we will see, opinions are often unreliable data to inform decisions, especially so when people are projecting future opinions about a thing that doesn't exist. This risk of a difference between what players say they will do, and what they will actually do means the usefulness of this data is low. Part of being a user researcher includes identifying which conclusions are safe, and which are risky, and making sure the development team understands this too.

The first step of development work before, or immediately after a green light, is often creating a 'vertical slice' - a representative section of the game which demonstrates the full experience in high fidelity. This is done to help decide whether to continue making the whole game. This is common when working with external funders or marketing teams, who need to be convinced that it will be worth the significant production cost. An example that Ninja Theory have shared comes from the creation of *Hellblade*[2]. They decided to create a vertical slice to explore not only how the game would feel to play, and demonstrate the core **loop** of gameplay, but also to learn how long it would take them to create content, so they could extrapolate how long making the whole thing would be.

There are some challenges with making vertical slices, and not every studio will do so. Although creating a representative experience of a game will only require a small section of level design content to be created, some other systems such as the combat system, controls and interface will need to be almost complete and require a lot of work to prepare. This means that although a vertical slice represents only a small part of the content, it doesn't represent a small part of the effort required to make games. They can be expensive and take a long time to produce.

If a team does create a vertical slice, this is a great opportunity to run research studies to help improve the quality of the final game. Usability testing, ensuring that players understand how it works and how to play it, can be run on this near-final quality experience. Identifying these issues early on before the game enters full production will help ensure designers understand the problems and

---

[2] Hellblade. 2017. Vertical Slice. [ONLINE] Available at: https://www.hellblade.com/vertical-slice/. [Accessed 12 June 2020].

have an opportunity to address them during the production
of the real experience.

Pre-production: Exploring the core experience

Creating a vertical slice will give an indication of how long a game will
take to make. This allows the full schedule to be planned out, and the
game to enter pre-production.

During pre-production, the core features will be made, as well as
representative assets - the levels, the character models, etc. At the end
of this period, the game will be playable but will still be rough and lack
polish, and will need significant iteration later in production.

User researchers can have a significant impact early in pre-production.
Since each feature or mechanic is being created and iterated upon
during this phase, research studies can ensure that the features are
understood, or experienced by players as intended. This is commonly
one to one studies, where a researcher observes a single player play
the game, and identifies usability issues.

This stage is also an opportunity to try out different gameplay ideas,
and discover whether they are worth investing more time and effort
on. This can involve both one to one studies and studies with multiple
participants simultaneously. These studies can focus on iterating the
core mechanics or exploring different ways of applying them to
identify the best possible implementation of the game.

The same is true for level design and scenarios (for example designing
an encounter with a new enemy). At this stage, designers have an
assumption about what players will do, what they will understand, and
how the encounter will play out. Creating studies that reliably uncover
player's real experiences with the scenario, or their ability to read
where they are meant to go on a level, will have a direct impact on
game design. Timing studies with when designers are working on each
feature will ensure that they are in a position to react to
research findings.

Once the game has all of the features added, this is often called an Alpha version.

Production: Scaling up and refining the experience

Once an acceptable Alpha version has been made, the whole game will exist and will be playable from start to finish. This is when the team size grows rapidly, and the product gets fleshed out and refined. Some studios start to open the game up to players at this point, particularly to focus on balancing difficulty to ensure it matches the intended experience.

For user researchers, there is a challenge with working on games later in production. Although it's often when studios will start to think about running research studies to 'see what players think', it can be too late to make significant changes. This can severely limit the impact of user research studies on the game's mechanics or design. If no further work is being done on level design, it may be too late to fix level design issues found in user research studies.

For user researchers, late in production will often be an appropriate time to run studies based on difficulty and balancing. This can include making sure that the players are able to progress through the whole thing, and that the amount of times they fail matches the experience intended by the designer. These long studies can often be multi-seat tests, where multiple players are playing through a game simultaneously, and a researcher uses a combination of **observation**, surveys and metrics reported by the game to identify parts that are easier, or harder, than intended.

Launch and after launch

A finished game can be known as going gold - named for the gold colour of writable CDs during the days when games were released on CDs. Traditionally this would be the point when it is too late to make further changes to the game, but this is no longer the case. Fast internet connections and release day patches now mean that studios can continue to use the time between sending a game for manufacturing, and the release date to make changes.

The concept of games as a service - providing a rolling programme of content updates for months or years after launch, has increased this trend. A prominent example is the continual content updates for *Fortnite,* advertised as seasons. This creates the opportunity for user research to continue to be relevant after a game is launched.

As will be covered later in the book, one of the challenges that impacts games more than other sectors is the desire for secrecy. Very expensive marketing strategies make studios worried about leaks, and cautious about putting their games in front of players during development for fear of the contents being shared on the internet. After launch, this becomes less of a barrier to running research, and there's more opportunity to be open about the game's contents - however a lot less opportunity to make changes as a result of testing, reducing the usefulness of testing.

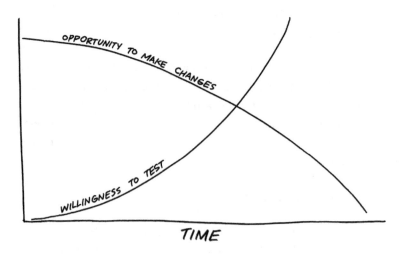

As development continues, teams are happier to test - but are less able to make changes

Post-launch usability and balancing testing may be most appropriate for genres that are more obviously iterative - mobile and free to play games will often be more open to these kinds of studies than traditional boxed experiences.

Match research studies to the team's current priorities

Although many studios do not follow exactly this process, or have different names for the stages, similar opportunities for research exist throughout development. As a user researcher, it's important to be aware of what your colleagues are working on, to identify where a research study can be most impactful

Many teams will be unfamiliar with all of the ways in which studies can help, and so education throughout the development process will be necessary. The role of being a user researcher is not just running studies but also evangelising and improving colleagues' understanding of how research works, by finding ways to demonstrate how it can improve the quality of experiences. Some techniques for doing this are covered later in this book.

WHO MAKES GAMES

There are many roles needed to make a game, and in smaller teams the same person can end up doing more than one of them. As a games user researcher, it's important to understand what your colleagues do, in order to ensure that findings get to the right person. It's no use telling the sound designer about issues with the level's layout.

In this chapter, we'll look at each person's role and the ways a user researcher might interact with them. Building strong relationships with colleagues is essential to running impactful user research studies. Some techniques for achieving this are covered in the second section of the book.

Game Designers

Game designer is a very broad term, which covers many specialisms - in some teams, one person might be doing many of these roles - in others, each will be a distinct individual or team. Some of the specialisms that a games designer may have include:

Level Design

Level designers create the environments that the player explores, and the scenarios they will encounter within those environments. This requires both planning what the levels, scenarios and characters will be, and using a level editing tool to shape the world and place characters within it, as well as determining the actions that each character will do.

Level and scenario design benefits hugely from user research studies. The designer has an expectation for how the player will react, and what they will do in the situation the level designer has created. By running sessions where real players are exposed to the scenario, it will identify areas where the current experience doesn't match how the designer wanted it to work - perhaps the player fails to understand which way to go, or doesn't see a key character they are meant to interact with. Researchers should work closely with designers while they create levels and scenarios. Running usability and gameplay studies to make sure the scenarios work as expected, and creating the opportunity to make changes to fix the experience, are some of the most impactful studies researchers can run.

Narrative Design

Many games have stories, and part of a game designer's role is to ensure that the story is understood and experienced by players as expected. As with level design, this role can involve both deciding what the story will be, and delivering the story in-game, through dialogue, environment or the scenarios a player encounters.

Successful narrative design requires communication with players to make sure that they have understood the story, their characters' motivations, and what is happening. This is also a very important area to run usability testing. Studies can ensure that players have understood the narrative that designers are trying to convey correctly, which will require putting players in front of the game, and then testing their understanding after they have been through it. These studies can inspire changes to how the narrative is communicated to address misunderstandings or fix bits that players missed.

Sound Design

Sound is a core part of the game's experience. This includes the music, sound effects and dialogue. These combine to create the emotional experience and also communicate information to the players - from which character is evil, to whether flicking that switch had any effect.

It may be rare for sound designers to commission research studies. Despite this, the usability issues that occur are often relevant to sound designers - either when issues are caused by sound effects, or could be fixed by using sound to prompt players. Because of this, make sure that sound designers are aware of the research studies being run, and are involved in the debrief of findings.

Game Artists

Games require a lot of custom art to be created. This is not just the interface (which is often done by UI artists) but also the models within the game - the characters, enemies, weapons, and objects in the world.

As with sound design, artists often want to communicate information to the players. For example, encouraging players to recognise a big glowing part on the boss as a weak point to aim at, or to notice when they are low on health.

This again is an area where usability studies will reveal the issue of players failing to recognise what the game is trying to communicate to them. It will be an artist's responsibility to fix many of the issues that are uncovered in testing. Ensuring that artists are aware when studies are running and are exposed to the findings will help make sure that the issues identified are fixed. Some techniques for increasing awareness of when studies are running are covered in the latter section of this book.

Producers

Producers make sure that the team has a shared vision of what needs to be done, and by when. They also check everyone has done their job so that the game comes together at the right time. Sometimes this role can be called a project manager, and the difference between the two roles can be nuanced in some companies. Producers will have a strong awareness of what everyone is working on, and be focused on prioritising where people's focus is to ensure that the game is completed. Similar roles can include development manager or development directors.

As a user researcher, producers are often one of the main roles that you will be working with. Producers are often the ones who commission research because they have a view of the development timeline and can identify the best moments where action can be taken to fix issues. Involving producers in the debrief process from research studies is very important since user research findings often create new tasks for others to do. Without the buy-in of a producer to prioritise and allocate these tasks, the study will have no impact on the game, wasting everyone's time.

Programmers

Programmers are software engineers who work in games. They write the code which controls how the game works and implement the systems within the game. There are often many specialities within programming, such as people who focus on physics, AI, graphics or networking. Many of these will be working closely with the other disciplines - designers, artists, and producers, to ensure that the team's shared vision is implemented correctly.

Programmers rarely commission research. Instead, they work very closely with the quality assurance team, who are looking for when the game isn't working as intended due to technical issues, rather than due to design issues. However, resolving usability and user experience issues will usually create some work for programmers. Because of this, it's important they are involved in discussions about how to resolve the issues uncovered during researcher studies.

User research studies might also require custom versions of the game to be produced, required for running a robust study. This will also require collaboration between programmers and user researchers.

Quality Assurance (QA)

QA looks for bugs in the software, where the game isn't working as intended. This involves playing through the game, understanding how it is meant to work, and identifying where the game isn't working as intended.

It's a role that can sometimes be confused with user research because user researchers are looking for issues in the game also. QA is looking for errors in how it has been implemented, whereas user researchers are looking for errors where the game has been implemented correctly, but that the implementation doesn't create the intended player experience. Explaining the difference between these two disciplines may be one of the early tasks a new user research team will have to do.

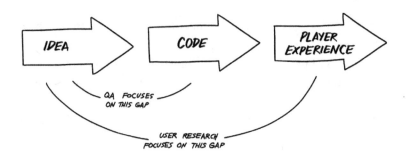

Although they work in similar areas, the focus of QA and User Research is different

QA people may also have usability feedback because they spend a lot of time playing the game and so will experience parts that are hard to understand or hard to do. Their feedback is a great indication of where potential issues might exist that can be explored further. It's worth remembering though that someone employed to work in quality assurance is going to be significantly different from an average player. They understand how the game works, and also are likely to be much more experienced with playing games than a person playing at home for the first time. Because of this, there will be a difference between the experience a QA person has, and the experience players will have, and it's still very important to run research studies with real participants.

Working well with QA can be a very productive relationship for user researchers, because they often have the best understanding of how to get the game running and the state of different **builds**, and can be a great help in preparing for a study. When running user research studies, it's common that some bits of the game won't be ready or working as intended. The QA team are most likely to know what isn't working, and how to work around it - essential for designing a study.

People who make tools

Many of these roles described don't write code themselves, and instead use design or scripting software to make assets for the game or decide how the game will work and render their intent within the game. One of the under-explored areas that a user researcher can have a huge impact on is in improving those tools a studio uses internally to create games. This involves running internal studies with their colleagues as participants, in collaboration with the people who make the tools, to make game development software easier to use and work more efficiently.

Working with internal tools developers, and running studies on how their tools are used can create goodwill, since improving tools will make colleagues' jobs easier. It will also improve the game. By speeding up development, and optimising workflows, more productive work can be done, and this can have a huge impact on the quality of the final game. It also will give the researcher more insight into the process of game development, helping them identify the most impactful studies they could be running.

Because the participants are internal - your colleagues - rather than members of the public, there can be some logistical challenges with running these kinds of studies. Because colleagues can't be paid for participation, scheduling and recruitment rely on goodwill and take a lot longer.

Others...

Game development can be messy, and people's responsibilities often don't neatly divide to exactly match the roles described above. The above roles are not a comprehensive list of all of the disciplines that exist within games.

To increase the impact of your user research studies, it's a good idea to spend time understanding the studios you work with, what people do and what decisions they are making. This involves a lot of meeting colleagues and talking to them, as well as participating in their team rituals - such as stand-up meetings, prioritisation sessions, or planning for milestones. Using this information to continually decide 'what is the most useful study that could be run at this time' will help ensure that research studies are relevant and findings are not ignored.

WHAT IS HARD ABOUT MAKING GAMES?

Game development can be difficult. Understanding some of the pressures that developers are under will make it possible to work out what studies will have the most impact, and when to run them.

Crunch

One of the most pressing challenges is finishing a game on time. Deadlines are sometimes decided years in advance and then locked in by purchasing advertising space. Advertising can be tremendously expensive - some reports say that the amount spent on advertising can often be equal to the cost of development for big AAA games[3]. On mobile games, the advertising cost is often far in excess of the development cost, because of the heavy competition in that field, and the costs of acquiring each user are closely monitored

As a consequence, missing a deadline for the marketing campaign isn't easy - it could be as expensive as developing the whole game again. This means that the title has to be finished on time.

Planning a game's development timeline can be difficult. Games are complex systems. It can be difficult to anticipate how long development of each part will take, while leaving enough time to fix bugs. This is easier with franchises, where the team have experience with previous iterations in the series and have a good idea about how long each part will take. Games with yearly updates, like *FIFA*, are an example of that. Other games are entirely new, and it's often not possible to tell how long developing each aspect will take until you're halfway through it, which makes forward planning very difficult.

This means that titles frequently slip from their intended development timeline and are at risk of not meeting their launch date. To make up the gap, studios start to '**crunch**' - requiring their employees to work

---

3 Venture Beat. 2018. The cost of games. [ONLINE] Available at: https://venturebeat.com/2018/01/23/the-cost-of-games/. [Accessed 12 June 2020]

longer hours, or on weekends, in order to try and make up the gap caused by inaccurate planning.

Crunch is unpopular, and perhaps not a good idea (tired people will make more mistakes and eventually extra work becomes unproductive). Despite this, it still occurs in many studios - particularly the larger ones with expensive marketing budgets, untested new features, or a lot of content.

As a user researcher, you may be asked to pull fewer all-night sessions than some other disciplines - it's hard to schedule a participant to come in at 3 am - but crunch might still mean long days to analyse and turn around reports faster.

Crunch can also impact a research team in other ways. It frequently leads to content or features being dropped or deferred for post-launch updates. Ensuring that the research team is in the loop with these discussions and using this information to prioritise their studies will be essential to ensuring studies are relevant and are the most impactful they can be.

Another more human impact is recognising that colleagues will be tired and under a lot of stress during crunch. This might impact how you decide to approach them - with patience and goodwill!

Keeping the secret

Another part of working in games to be aware of is the importance of secrecy. As mentioned previously, studios spend a lot of money on marketing so have carefully planned roadmaps of what information will be shared publicly and when this will be shared to create the biggest buzz around the game.

Leaks which reveal information early disrupt these plans and potentially have an impact on how successful the game will be. To avoid this, studios ensure non-public information is kept confidential. This is particularly a risk for games user research - studies typically involve bringing members of the public in, and they have more temptation to leak secrets.

Keeping information secret can be difficult as people are passionate about games, and want to talk about them. As someone working in games, it's necessary to be very careful about discussing games prior to launch - including on CV & portfolios. There are many news stories about information being leaked accidentally by people updating their profile on LinkedIn, which could put the brakes on a career in games.

For research participants, it's common to ask them to sign a non-disclosure agreement, NDA, prior to taking part in a study. This is a document that confirms they agree not to talk about what they have seen or done during the study - sometimes until the game's launch, sometimes ever. The existence of the NDA may also help convince colleagues worried about leaks that research studies can be run safely.

Creating disposable versions of a game

Teams often have to create things other than the final game they are working on. Throughout development, there will be times when it's necessary to show progress to people - whether it's investors checking in on the game they are funding, or at big shows or announcements.

The real in-progress game is often not in an appropriate state to be shown at these events, which require the code to run well and look like a complete experience. This means that custom development work is required to create a playable, or semi-playable version of the game to demo at trade shows or to investors. A lot of the work to create those builds is bespoke and doesn't help progress towards completing the final game. This distracts teams from developing the experience for real.

As a user researcher, these semi-playable builds may be suitable for running usability testing and uncovering higher-fidelity findings than the real game is in a state to learn about. It also can require some additional studies - these builds are often for high profile events, and running usability tests to inform the development of them will help the demos be successful.

Worrying about job security

As covered in the 'games are a business' section, there are times where a full team may not be required. Studios try to plan for this by having multiple games in development simultaneously, but this isn't always successful - delays such as cancelled projects, development slowing down or failing to get funding will lead to times when a full development team isn't required.

Because of this, layoffs are common, and there is less job security than in many other industries. This is particularly difficult as mass-layoffs means that all of your former colleagues will also be job hunting, flooding the market and making it harder to get another job due to the sudden increase in competition.

This is a risk to most disciplines in games development, and user researchers are no exception. When working with studios with less mature research practice, people might question the usefulness of keeping user researchers at stages of game development when usability studies are less relevant. This can make a user research role less stable than content creation roles, such as artists.

Sometimes the situation is so dire that nothing can be done and job losses are inevitable. As user researchers, we also believe that we can run relevant studies throughout the whole lifecycle of game development. Spending time educating colleagues about the potential for research studies, and evangelising for player-centric decision making throughout development can help reduce the risk that the role is seen as optional when times are lean. Talking about the business benefits of running user research studies - that we can help teams reach their design goals quicker - will help make the financial case that user research is a worthwhile investment through development.

SUMMARISING HOW GAMES GET MADE

In this section, we've covered some of the basics about how games get made, who does it, and the challenges games developers face.

User research is a support role which makes game development easier through running useful studies to inform and evaluate design decisions. This will help teams get to the best implementation quicker, reducing the financial and time pressure studios are under. This gives them freedom to tackle and solve more interesting design problems and make better player experiences.

In the next part of the book, we'll cover what a user researcher actually does, and how to run studies that make games better.

PART 2

HOW TO RUN GAMES USER RESEARCH STUDIES

Not every studio employs games user researchers. Those that do might have a different job title for the role - a common synonym is **UX Researcher**, the job it describes is the same.

An adjacent discipline is UX Designer, who may run user research studies as part of their role but will also be responsible for the changes made to the game based on what was learned in the study. Although they don't have the same singular focus on running studies that a dedicated user researcher has, they apply many of the same skills to perform their duties.

Regardless of the job title, games user researchers evaluate and inspire game design decisions, by designing, running, analysing and debriefing studies with players.

In this section, we'll explore how to be a user researcher and how this fits in with the rest of the development process. As an introduction, we'll explain each part of the job description in turn to give an overview of the role:

Evaluate game design decisions

Making games requires many decisions, including:

- What features will be in a game

- How should those features be implemented

- How should that feature be taught

- How do we signal to players when to use the feature

Good game design has intent behind each of these decisions, and doesn't let them happen by accident. A designer may think 'we would like to make a special move that allows players to push back groups of enemies when they are overwhelmed, so that they have the opportunity to use their one to one combat abilities'. Teams then make decisions about implementation in order to create that experience within the game.

However it can be difficult to tell whether their decisions have had the correct outcome. Has the designer successfully:

- Taught players how to activate the special move?

- Taught players when the special move is appropriate to activate?

- Taught players when they should not be using that special move?

- Convinced players the special move is worth using?

- Ensured that players are physically able to activate the special move when required?

A key part of being a user researcher is to run studies that answer those questions, and ensure the game is experienced as the designer intended.

Inspire game design decisions

Many design decisions are improved by understanding how players really behave. Watching real players experience prototypes, or understanding their behaviour with other games reveals the best implementation quicker than going through cycles of guessing and making changes until arriving at the best solution.

These types of studies can inspire new ideas and solutions - they allow designers to observe emergent gameplay in prototypes and discover where the fun is. It can also include competitor research, looking at what we can learn from how players experience other games, to inform the development of something new.

Researchers also run studies which investigate the player's environment - particularly relevant when making mobile games which can be played anywhere, or active games which require players to move around a physical space. A better understanding of the player's situation and previous experience will be able to inspire the design of features for them.

In games, this type of research is less commonly run than **evaluative research** such as usability testing, often experienced designers want to take a shot at a solution based on gut-feel or intuition rather than asking for information beforehand. This can be due to their confidence in their professional expertise, their pride making it difficult to ask for research, or simply a lack of time to run the right study. When they are run, these types of studies will save time, and development cost, by getting to the best solution quicker.

Designing studies

There are many different ways in which studies can be run, with a range of methods to be used, questions that can be asked, or tasks that can be set. Ensuring the correct ones are selected so that the study answers the team's research questions is a user researcher's job.

Designing studies also requires a lot of organisation - ensuring that the players turn up, that they are the right kind of players, that the game code will be ready on time - to make sure the study runs as planned. These responsibilities are also part of a user researcher's role.

Running studies

Running studies is the part where the study generates data. Responsibilities include moderating the session - interacting directly with the players to ensure the session goes as planned. It will also include note-taking, or other data collection activities, observing things that occur that are worthy of note, and capturing them for future analysis.

Analysing studies

After completing a study, there is a lot of raw data that has been generated. This can include videos of people playing, notes about what happened during the study, survey responses from participants or analytics captured by the game. The researcher will then have to sort through this raw data, interpret it, and come to some conclusions about what the answers to the research objectives are.

Debriefing studies

Having found some answers, the researcher is responsible for sharing that information with the right people, who are responsible for making game design decisions. Ensuring that the issues are understood and get to the right person is part of the responsibility of a researcher. Some researchers will also use this as an opportunity to draw upon their expertise about player behaviour to help fix the issues observed in their studies.

With players

Game developers are not the same as other players - they have a lot more background information about game design, and the specific experience being tested, which means it wouldn't be a fair test if they were the subject of the study. Most research studies require finding real people who would play the game in real life, and using them as the participants for the study. Finding the right participants, and checking that the participants represent real players, is part of a user researcher's responsibility.

This section of the book probes on each of these responsibilities in depth. At the end of this section, you will know how to explain what a games user researcher does and be ready to plan and run reliable studies which inform game design decisions.

GAMES USER RESEARCHERS DON'T...

User research is new to many smaller studios, and colleagues may not be clear on what exactly it is a user researcher does. As well as understanding what user researchers do, it's also helpful to anticipate some common misconceptions about what user research is. This will help explain the role to colleagues inexperienced at working with user researchers.

User researchers don't do market research

There is a field of research called market research, which uses methods such as focus groups and surveys to identify trends in consumer behaviour and anticipate whether people will purchase something. This can be used for judging people's opinions of different potential game ideas, or uncovering their thoughts on existing games, and can be impactful early in the development process. Game studios or publishers may commission market research to inform a design brief, about what type of game will be made, or identify how to advertise it once created.

These types of studies are often controversial and thought to be compromising the artistic vision of games. Some consider these studies to alter the creative team's vision to chase a popular idea. This is seen as not authentic, or morally impure compared to creating art for art's sake. In contrast a user researcher often try to avoid this association and frame their work as helping the team's ideas be understood and experienced by players as the creator intended.

Market research is not what a user researcher will be doing. Although much of the terminology is similar, user researchers will be running deep studies looking at people's behaviour and should be very careful if asked to run studies to identify gaps in the market.

There can often be areas where the objectives of a user research study are very close to market research, such as when exploring opinions, and the differences between the two disciplines can sometimes be fuzzy. Despite many articles explaining that user research and market research are different, a lot of the reasons these articles suggest may not stand up to scrutiny - they commonly include describing the difference as being quantitative (research focused on analysing numerical data) vs qualitative (research focused on analysing text, verbal or visual data), when really both disciplines employ both methods based on the objectives of a study.

Perhaps some of the clearest distinctions that do exist include how the researchers seek to describe and segment players - market researchers will typically segment by demographic or spending habits, user researchers by behaviour. Their outlook may also be different - user researchers are more likely to tell teams what's wrong with the game, market researchers will focus on what's going well.

Regardless, it's safest for user researchers to be clear about the type of studies they do run, and the value these bring, to avoid confusion or conflict with market research teams. User researchers are very experienced with behavioural objectives - such as 'can players get through the game?' and, 'do players experience the game as intended?' Starting a new relationship with studies in these areas can help clarify the value user research brings, particularly with studios who are new to research, before delving into more advanced studies.

User researchers don't design

The goal of running user research studies is to empower designers to make better decisions and to evaluate whether their decisions have had the intended effect. The role of a user researcher is not to make those decisions themselves.

This means we have to understand what the designer's intention is before we can do our job, and shouldn't be deciding that intent ourselves. We can then run studies that look at the gap between the **design intent,** and what has actually been made.

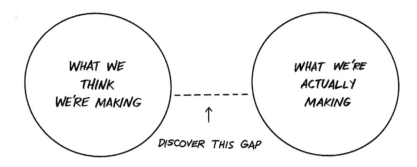

There is a gap between what game studios think they are making, and what players actually experience. Research studies reveal this.

For example, if a designer wants to introduce the new special ability previously described to push enemies back, researchers will run studies to learn whether players can use the ability, and whether they understand how it works. However, researchers will not decide whether that special ability should be in the game, or what to do if players' can't use the special ability.

User researchers focus on discovering the problems, not deciding what to do about them.

This can sometimes be tricky, and it's tempting for user researchers to try and sneak their ideas in - particularly when describing the cause of issues they've found. 'Players didn't learn how to use the special move because of the lack of the tutorial,' looks like it's describing the problem but is sneakily also a design solution. Watch out for accidentally suggesting a solution ('there should be a tutorial') when trying to describe the problem.

Giving design recommendations makes keeping this separation between understanding the problems and describing solutions challenging. Many design teams ask their researcher for recommendations - 'how do you think the problem should be fixed?'

This can be risky to answer. Although researchers are often experts in what occurred during their studies, they lack the specialist domain knowledge that a designer, programmer or product manager would have. This can include knowing what options are available to resolve the issue, what can be done in the time available, what is technically feasible in this game engine or what has been tried before. Instead, I strongly recommend a collaborative approach for coming up with solutions, rather than just providing design recommendations. A technique for doing this is covered later in the Debriefing a Study section of this book.

The risk with going ahead and giving design solutions is that it dilutes the impact of other user research insight. People must be able to trust that the findings from a study are true - it is an undeniable fact that some players failed to learn how to use the special ability. However, decisions about what to do about it are subjective and based on the researcher's opinion - 'We should make a prompt flash whenever the special ability should be used'. By giving both types of feedback together, colleagues may confuse the true research findings with opinion, which can lead to findings being dismissed and reduce the impact of the study.

Neutrality is, therefore, a key part of being a games user researcher - being evidence-led and avoiding subjective opinions about design decisions will help create trust in the truth of their research findings.

User researchers don't make games easier

Making a game easy doesn't usually make it fun. In many other types of software, making tasks efficient is a way of reducing frustration - no-one wants to spend 30 minutes trying to order a taxi via an app. In contrast, with games efficiency isn't the goal - otherwise, Mario could be replaced with a button like this:

An example of a very easy game

Instead, the goal of research studies is to ensure that the player's experience matches what the designer wanted it to be. This means there are two types of difficulty that players can experience.

Designed difficulty is parts that are intentionally difficult, and that the challenge has been intentionally crafted by a designer. Previous work, like Raph Koster's *Theory of Fun for Game Design* describes that encountering challenge, and then overcoming it, is a key part of what makes games fun[4]. Creating difficulty is crucial for designers in order to make games fun.

Undesigned difficulty is when the challenge isn't intentional, and the player finds something difficult that they weren't meant to find difficult - or something easy that wasn't meant to be easy. This can often be due to usability issue - for example, the game doesn't succeed in telling players where to go, or what they are meant to do. When that isn't what the designer wanted, this kind of difficulty isn't helpful and disrupts the intended experience.

The goal of a user researcher is to reduce the undesigned difficulty so that only the designed difficulty is experienced by the player. This means that the player experience can then be curated. The designer can correctly anticipate how difficult players will find each part - giving them the power to pace out the difficulty and combine exciting moments with calmer points to create a great experience.

User researchers don't stop art

Games are an artistic medium. A concern some people might have is that introducing information learned from user research into the design process might compromise the integrity of games as an artistic medium.

This is often based on an incorrect assumption about the type of information that research studies reveals, and how that information is handled. The most reliable type of information that a user research study reveals is behavioural - such as whether players could do the things the designer hoped they could do, and, if not, why they failed. Instead, people imagine focus groups and market research studies with findings such as 'kids like skateboarding, so make the game's hero a skateboarder'. This is not what user researchers do.

The goal from research studies is to ensure that the artistic vision from designers is received correctly by the player, not to change the

---

[4] Koster, R., 2013. Theory of Fun for Game Design. 2nd ed: O'Reilly Media.

designer's artistic vision. The studies run by researchers will support art rather than stop it.

User researchers don't guarantee success

Unfortunately making fun and usable games aren't the only element needed for success. Marketing spend is probably just as important. Big games such as *Destiny*, *Heavy Rain* and *Call of Duty* spent more on marketing than on the development of the game, and advertising was a key part of achieving sales. This is even more true in mobile gaming, where advertising costs greatly outweigh development costs.

User research does promise to reduce the risk of failure. One reason a game might fail is due to players not enjoying it, or not understanding it. User research can fix those issues and improve the game's odds - but not guarantee success, which is a shame.

WORKING WITH OTHERS

In the first section of this book, some of the professions who make games were introduced. As a user researcher, there are some disciplines you collaborate with more often when running studies - usually the relationships where it's obvious how research studies inform their decisions - such as producers, designers, and artists.

Building relationships with these colleagues is essential to running impactful studies. To do this, it's helpful to understand how research works with game teams and how to make research findings understood.

Where research sits in a game team

There is no best model for how research works within a studio. The right way of working depends on factors such as the studio's current projects, their previous experience with researchers (which isn't always positive) and their understanding of the variety of ways user research can be integrated into the development of games. There are two more common setups that a user research team might have - a centralised model, or an embedded model.

In a centralised model, there is one user research team who runs studies when agreed in partnership with the game team. In this model, all of the researchers would typically be sat together, and consider their team to be the other researchers. This can be more common for research teams based at game publishers, where the researchers are responsible for more than one game at a time, or when the user research team is actually an external agency commissioned for individual studies.

The centralised model has some benefits. As there is only one team of researchers, it is easier to create a research community, sharing knowledge, processes and tools, and collaborating with peer researchers to assess and improve how research works to support game development. Working with multiple teams can also help with job security during lean periods.

However, this model also distances the researchers from the rest of the development team - such as designers and producers - reducing their exposure to where and when decisions get made. This risks researchers not being in the room when there are debates about the game's priorities or where to focus people's time, which creates missed opportunities where a research study could have helped, but no-one thought to do it. Building strong relationships with producers, who have oversight over current priorities, is essential to overcome this shortcoming.

An alternate model, more common in studios dedicated to a single title, is having the researcher embedded with the rest of the game team. In this model, they sit with people from other disciplines, rather than with other researchers. In contrast to the centralised model, this gives researchers greater access to people and decision making. By following closely what colleagues are working on, there are more opportunities to run relevant studies that the team might not have thought to commission themselves, or to remind people of the results of previous studies at opportune times. This can greatly increase the impact that research studies can have.

However, this embedded model forces a user researcher to be the sole representative of user research, and lessens their exposure to research peers. This can cause stagnation - failing to learn new things - and a lack of oversight which might let poorer-quality studies slip through. When working in an embedded model, a researcher might need to more actively seek out mentoring or support from an external community of researchers to ensure that they continue to develop and critique their research skills.

Neither model is 'correct', and many studios use a combination of both - being part of a centralised research team, while attending key game team meetings. A user researcher's ultimate goal is to be responsive to the needs of the team to make games better. A flexible approach to ways of working is required to avoid distractions and focus on what is best for the development of the game.

Building relationships with game teams

One of the most important skills for a user researcher to succeed, beyond running good studies, is being able to communicate well and build relationships with colleagues. User researchers don't make design decisions themselves and only support the decision making of others, so they need to work well with colleagues to have any significant impact.

Decision makers are not just the people with designer in their title. Dedicating time to understand who is making design decisions about the game will make it easier to help colleagues understand how user research can support them, and when they should be running studies. It will also allow a user researcher to more accurately assess the impact of their studies, and prioritise research requests appropriately.

This work is as valuable as running high-quality studies. If a researcher is doing great work, but no-one is looking at it, there's no point running these studies. Building trust is a long term project, and some steps researchers can take to help grow trust and confidence in research are covered later in this book.

There is a temptation for researchers to use complicated academic language to give the impression that they are experts. Done to excess, this is alienating to colleagues, and won't endear you to others. It will also lead to findings being misunderstood. Writing in plain english, using short, uncomplicated words with a clear structure will make it easier for teams to understand and apply research findings to their own work.

Of course, people are different and may have different preconceptions about user research. Some will embrace the opportunity to request studies with open arms, recognising the value it brings to game development. Others will view it as a challenge to their ability to do their job, or assume it's just asking people if they like the game and brings no value. In interactions with all game development colleagues, remember that no-one is trying to be a bad person. Spending time listening to them to understand their priorities, motivations and previous experience will help frame the benefits of running studies and increase the impact of user research.

HOW IS GAMES USER RESEARCH DIFFERENT TO OTHER TYPES OF USER RESEARCH?

User research doesn't just exist for games, and is well established in other types of software development. Many people move into the games industry from working as a user researcher in other industries such as creating software, apps or websites, and vice versa. New perspectives from other industries can be very valuable to help encourage diversity in thought and approach and move the field forward.

Although I believe that the differences aren't huge between user research in games, and user research elsewhere, it's worth considering what they are. The biggest challenge for someone transitioning into games user research can be having the domain knowledge - understanding enough about current games to be able to interact with other professionals and participants sensibly and explain research findings appropriately.

Objectives

In most software, efficiency is important and correlates strongly with users' opinions about how good an experience it is. No-one wants to spend thirty minutes using an app to book a taxi if it could take five seconds. However, efficiency is less relevant for many games - people presumably have a better time spending thirty minutes slaying the dragon than if it was over in five seconds.

As well as how long an experience takes, difficulty is also different for games. People don't want to have to overcome puzzles or work out the best strategy for ordering their taxi, whereas a game without challenge is unlikely to be fun.

This means that typical usability objectives for software such as 'is it quick to complete,' and 'can people get through it without encountering issues,' are not relevant for games.

As a consequence, the research objectives from a game can often be more nuanced than those of other software and should explore whether the challenges that players encounter were the intended ones the designers created, or whether they were unintended challenges. It then requires further exploration for those unintended challenges - are they serendipitous things the designer would like to encourage, or are they problems that need to be fixed. This makes 'fun' one of the common questions that a team might have about their game, and much more valuable than 'how long did it take to complete'. Measuring fun isn't easy, which we'll come back to later.

Methods

Some of the methods that are commonly used for user research have some differences when applied for games user research. There are a few reasons for this. Because the objectives of games user research studies are different, the methods used to uncover those objectives will also have to be changed. Many games achieve most of their sales immediately after launch, which makes some post-launch methods impractical, like A/B testing. Other factors that might impact the method choice is the emphasis on secrecy that games have over other sectors, which makes running remote research without supervising participants more challenging. The multiplayer experience is also often an important part of games, and requiring multiple people to use the software simultaneously is more common than in other sectors - leading to different methodological choices.

These factors combine to have an impact on both what methods are picked, and how they are adapted for use in games. Remote testing, where the participants take part from home using screen sharing or streaming, although not impossible, is less common due to the challenges of preventing leaks occurring. Games user research also commonly uses fusions of both qualitative and quantitative methods. Lots of people playing simultaneously in a large research lab are often used to recreate realistic multiplayer setups, or to allow quantitative questions to be explored, such as measuring difficulty. Methods are explored in more depth later in this book.

Research maturity

In the 1970's, Atari hired Carol Kantor to help evaluate whether their in-development games would be successful, using a combination of observation, surveys and focus groups[5]. Despite this early start, the application of user-centred design processes into games development has been slower than in some other fields.

This means at many studios their understanding of the potential for user research studies can be limited. It's commonly assumed that user research is just usability testing, missing the opportunity for research to inform design decisions as they are made. Although this problem isn't limited to user research in games, it is common at many game studios. This can be exacerbated in studios which currently run playtests as informal feedback sessions, who may not understand the difference between those tests, and a robust and reliable research study.

Many studios may not see the relevance of user research early in development, or after a game is launched. Addressing this requires active engagement with the other disciplines, and creating opportunities to evangelise and educate people about research.

This lack of research maturity can also lead to the idea that games need to be ready to test. This can happen due to a lack of trust in the researcher's ability to work around parts that are not implemented yet to focus only on the relevant objectives, or because teams are worried that the results will embarrass them in front of their bosses. Waiting until a game is ready is always risky - once a feature is close to complete, there is political momentum, and development cost, behind it leading to resistance to making changes. As a user researcher, I've never run a study without finding issues - no matter how small the scope - and it is my belief that something useful can always be learned from studies, regardless of whether the game is 'ready'.

---

[5] Norman, K. and Kirakowski, J., 2017. The Wiley Handbook of Human Computer Interaction Set.: John Wiley & Sons

Later in this section of the book, we'll talk about some of the techniques a user researcher can use to help improve awareness of all of the ways they can support development teams throughout the development of a game, not just at the end.

PLANNING AND RUNNING RESEARCH STUDIES

The main thing a games user researcher does is plan and run studies that answer game design questions. This involves a number of steps to accomplish.

In some game studios, a single researcher does all of the steps required to run a study from end to end. In others, researchers have more specialised roles and will focus only on specific parts of the process - for example at Ubisoft where the tasks of planning a study and running the study are done by different people. However, in most places, a researcher is expected to be comfortable leading every part of a study.

In this section, we'll explore in turn all of the tasks that running a study entails, including:

- Defining research objectives

- Designing a games user research study

- The methods used for research

- Planning the admin required for a study, and recruiting participants

- Running a games user research study

- Analysing data from research studies

- Debriefing studies

By exploring each step in turn, we will cover the end-to-end running of a study, which will be typical of many games user research projects.

DEFINING RESEARCH OBJECTIVES

Every research study starts with the objectives, defining what the study is going to learn. These are based on the work being done by the rest of the game team - what decisions are they making, and what information do they need from a study to make those decisions easier.

A common mistake that researchers make is starting with the method (e.g. we're going to run a usability test), and then coming up with the objectives that fit that method. This can occur when researchers feel more comfortable with some methods than others. Unfortunately, picking the method first limits the types of objectives that can be reliably answered - for example, if the decision is made to run a usability test, the team won't be able to get high-quality answers around difficulty balancing. This can lead to running low impact studies that fail to address the questions that game teams really need answering. Always start by defining the objectives before deciding the method.

Some examples of potential research objectives include:

- Do players know where to go on level 2?

- Do players understand how to use fast-travel?

- Can players complete the puzzle in the right time?

- Does the tutorial teach players how to use their jetpack correctly?

- Is the difficulty correct?

- Do players enjoy the game?

Coming up with objectives should be a collaborative activity, defined by what the rest of the studio is working on currently. It's a bad sign if a researcher is coming up with objectives with no input from other team members, since it increases the risk of no-one being ready to react to the findings of the research study once it's complete.

Deciding research objectives is often done in a **kick-off meeting,** where potential objectives for each study can be discussed and agreed. Before the kick-off meeting, a researcher spends some time gathering potential objectives for a study from discussions with colleagues working in design or production. Researchers might also suggest some objectives based on their understanding of the current priorities in the game. These potential objectives can then be nuanced, prioritised and agreed in the kick-off meeting with leads representing different disciplines (level design, art design, producers, etc) to confirm the most useful things a study could focus on at that time.

It can be difficult to schedule time with all of the leads. On those occasions, spending time with a senior producer who can help give an overview of the state of the game can help, combined with 1:1 catch-ups with any other important leads.

As well as agreeing on the objectives, the kick-off meeting agenda should also cover:

- The players. What type of player is the game aimed at, and what attributes should the participants for this study have.

- The method. The researcher should give an indication of the appropriate research method to answer these objectives, with the caveat that this may change as the study design progresses.

- The study dates. Discuss and agree deadlines and dates, useful for producers who need to plan when to schedule changes based on the findings, or when additional development work is needed to create a testable version of the game.

- Who should be involved. Ask if there are any team members not present who the findings will be relevant for, and should be invited to view research sessions or attend the debrief.

- The build. Find out when the version of the game used for the test will be ready. It's recommended to put this deadline far enough in advance of the study to allow the build to be reviewed before the test, to give the researcher time to react if it's in a bad state.

By having a kick-off meeting, it ensures that all of the relevant disciplines are aware of upcoming studies, and have the opportunity to have their views and priorities included in decision making. This can have a big impact on the success of user research inside a studio.

After the meeting, the conclusions should be documented and shared - creating a document that records what the objectives are, and what was agreed around dates and team members. Any research objectives that aren't answerable in this study can also be captured, so that they can be answered later when appropriate. This document will be very valuable to the researcher when designing and planning the study.

Having successfully agreed the objectives from a study, it's now time to start designing what the study will actually be, and preparing for it.

DESIGNING A GAMES USER RESEARCH STUDY

Having gathered research objectives, a user researcher will then create a study that can answer them. This involves:

- Deciding the appropriate method or methods to use

- Creating the tasks or prompts that the player will be given

- Deciding how to capture data generated from the study

- Deciding how to analyse the data generated from the study

The study then gets written down in a **study plan** (or **discussion guide**), which can be shared with the game team and used by the researcher to guide their sessions.

Deciding the right method

Following the kick-off, a user researcher will have a list of objectives that the study would like to learn, such as:

- 'Do players learn how to use the jetpack?'

- 'Can players identify the correct strategy for defeating this boss, and beat it?'

- 'Is the difficulty correct?'

- 'How does the jump feel?'

- 'Is this multiplayer map balanced?'

- 'Do players discover the secondary mode for the weapon?'

- 'Do players know where to go for their next objective?'

- 'Do players like the chase sequence?'

These then need to be matched to the right method to answer them. The next chapter goes into methods in more depth, but one way of grouping them is:

- Behavioural Methods (which uncover what players are doing, whether players understand and can perform tasks as intended)

- Experiential Methods (which explore what players think about the game)

There's been a long-running debate in the research community about the correct way to describe these groupings, and so the language used will not be consistent across companies. Some synonyms for these are covered in the glossary.

Some of the example objectives given above are focused on whether a player understands or can do something. These are:

- 'Do players learn how to use the jetpack?'

- 'Can players identify the correct strategy for defeating this boss, and beat it?'

- 'Do players discover the secondary mode for the weapon?'

- 'Do players know where to go for their next objective?'

These objectives would be answered by observing players behaviour and asking questions to reveal their understanding or the behaviour observed. This can then help explain why players are failing to learn or use the abilities that the designer wanted them to.

Some of the objectives are focused on measuring the player's experience and comparing it to a predetermined goal.

These are:

- 'Is the difficulty correct?'

- 'Is this multiplayer map balanced?'

These would be answered by recording what happens in the game - for example, how many times the player dies, where those deaths are, or which starting position causes teams to win multiplayer games more often. They would then be compared to the experience the designer intended - such as how many times did the designer want the player to fail on this level.

Some of the objectives are based around what a player thinks about the game. These are:

- 'How does the jump feel?'

- 'Do players like the chase sequence?'

These would be answered by discovering what a player thinks, understanding why they think that, and then measuring what percentage of people agree with that opinion.

When planning a study, the user researcher will review each of the objectives in turn and decide what the appropriate approach would be to answer them. This is done by first categorising the type of research objective it is, and then deciding what method to use within that category. In a real-world games development environment, this requires a bit of pragmatism, and the ideal method might not be possible due to budget or time constraints. Remember that getting some quite good findings to a studio at the right time is much more useful than getting very good findings to the team too late. We look at some ways of speeding up the research process later in the book.

Prioritising the research objectives will also help with this. Sometimes a study requires different methods that cannot all be ran reliably in a single study. When this occurs work with colleagues to decide which research objectives are more important, and choose the method that best supports those objectives. This will help decide how to assign limited researcher time across mixed-method studies.

Creating the tasks

Having picked the method, the next step is to define how the research objective will be answered. Each research objective will require:

- The task or tasks that will be given to the player to create data

- The way data will be collected

Sometimes the task will seem obvious. If the research objective is 'can players complete the puzzle?', an obvious task would be 'get players to complete the puzzle.'. For some objectives, the task doesn't even need to be explicitly given to the participant - in longer playthroughs they could be asked to play the game, and the researcher can be alert for the sections they are interested in without prompting the player. This creates more natural behaviour, which is a good thing.

For other research objectives, more specific tasks may be appropriate for the player, such as directing them towards completing specific parts of the game. There are some traps to watch out for when giving defined tasks to players during research studies.

First, be careful about the wording of the task. The words used will impact a player's behaviour, and could give them information they might not already have had. For example saying 'please complete this puzzle' would reveal to players that a puzzle exists. If their issue had been that they didn't see the puzzle, or didn't understand it was a puzzle, that issue would then be lost because the researcher has revealed the puzzle exists. Being very nondescript when giving instructions to players is sensible, starting with broad tasks such as 'please play this section of the game', and carefully guiding further as required.

Another aspect to consider when designing the tasks is to recreate knowledge a player would have got from other sections of the game. If the study starts on level two, and misses the tutorials from level one, plenty of usability issues will be caused by missing the tutorials. This isn't a fair test, and is not creating useful findings - in the final game, players would have experienced the tutorial, and so any issues caused by missing the tutorial can be dismissed immediately. When writing tasks, make sure to consider what information a player would normally have by this point. Then give that information directly to players, so that the findings from a study are more representative of the real experience players would have. Often tutorials aren't ready until late in development but can be recreated artificially in a study by the moderator teaching participants the game's controls and features, or through written handouts. When learning the controls or mechanics aren't the objective of the study, introducing them manually allows other issues to be discovered.

Each research objective will require one or more tasks. Run through each objective, and decide what those tasks will be. These can then be ordered in a way that will make sense for the player, so that the session flows in a logical order. These can then be documented as part of creating the study plan.

Research Objective	Task
'Do players learn how to use the jetpack'	Complete the jetpack tutorial
'Do players discover the secondary mode for the weapon?'	Complete levels one and two
'Do players know where to go for their next objective?'	Complete levels one and two
'Can players identify the correct strategy for defeating this boss, and beat them?'	Complete the boss encounter

Each research objective will have at least one task associated with it. One task can answer more than one research objective (and vice versa!).

Deciding what data to collect

Each task that the player performs will be generating data about their behaviour and opinions, such as:

- What the player is doing in the game - where they go, what items they use, where they succeed and where they fail.

- What the player's opinion is, and why they are thinking that.

It is through capturing and understanding this data that the research objectives can be answered. When planning a study, it is necessary to anticipate what data will be generated, and how to collect it.

For each objective, think about how it could be measured. Some objectives are focused on performance or behaviour, and could be measured by observing what players are doing - are they able to complete the section? Do they know where to go? Do they get stuck for a long time? Observations can be performed either by the researcher, or from in-game analytics.

Other objectives are focused around a player's thoughts, such as do they enjoy the experience, does the player believe it's too easy or too hard, etc. This data can be captured by getting players to articulate their thoughts or opinions - either through asking them questions verbally, or asking for ratings or comments on a survey.

It's really important with all of these task measurements to make sure that the design intent is understood - what did the designer want the experience to be like. Depending on what the designer wants, dying three times on a level could mean it's too easy, just right, or too hard. There's no way to tell which is correct without understanding what the designer wanted to happen. It's also important to capture how this made players feel, to allow the designer to assess if their design idea creates the intended experience for players. As a researcher, for each of the things you intend to observe, be sure to define what a good or bad result would look like before the study begins.

It's also important to ensure that the data captured will give you enough detail to explain what you learned to the development team. As well as noting what occurred, also uncover and note why it occurred. This will require probing players to reveal the reason for their behaviour or opinion. Players may have failed to go the right way; without asking the right questions it won't be clear whether this is because they failed to see where to go, failed to understand it was where they were meant to go, or whether they understood it was the correct route, but had decided not to go that way for other reasons.

Some of the observations that a researcher should make can be anticipated in the study plan.

Research Objective	Task	How will we assess?
Do players learn how to use the jetpack?	Complete the jetpack tutorial	- Observe if they can complete the tutorial Ask them to demonstrate how tutorial works at end of session
Do players discover the secondary mode for the weapon?	Complete levels one and two	- Observe if they discover and use secondary mode - Ask players to explain secondary mode at end of session
Do players know where to go for their next objective?	Complete levels one and two	- Observe if players can successfully wayfind between objectives
Can players identify the correct strategy for defeating this boss, and beat them?	Complete the boss encounter	- Observe if players can defeat the boss - Ask player to explain boss strategy, and see if correct - Count failed attempts and compare to expected - Ask players to rate difficulty of the boss

Decide how data for each research objective will be collected, and what will be assessed

Defining what data will be captured, and how it will be obtained, will help prepare for the analysis stage later.

Documenting the plan

Having decided what tasks will be set to the player, and how the data will be collected, this can then be used to create the study plan (or discussion guide) which describes the study.

This document can be useful for multiple reasons. The first is that by creating the plan, it gives the researcher confidence that they have covered all of the objectives with appropriate tasks and that the study has no gaps.

Secondly, it can be used to guide the session itself, and the researcher can refer to it when running sessions to prompt them on the questions to ask. Lastly, it can be useful to show to others - note-takers or other researchers working on the study to encourage consistency between how the sessions run.

This can be created as a word document, using Google Docs or Microsoft Word. Some sections that may be useful to include, for referring to in the session, are:

- Recapping the research objectives

- The times sessions are booked for

- The running order of each session, for example:

  - Pre Interview

  - Task 1: Tutorial

  - Task 2: Introductory Level

  - Task 3: Car Chase Scene

  - Survey

  - Post Interview

- The introductory information for participants - e.g. explaining consent, the study, what data will be collected. This can often be templated, and more information is later in the book.

- The tasks and prompts that will be given to participants, with the data that will be captured, using the format described above.

- Scripts for pre- or post-session interviews

This can look something like this:

Pre Interview

- What games have you been playing recently?
- What do you think about (game they played?)
  - Anything you particularly like about it?
  - Anything you don't like?
- Have you ever heard of a game called 'UX Invaders'?
  - What have you heard about it

First Task - Tutorial

Task: Imagine you have just downloaded this game, and are playing it for the first time. Please play this tutorial level, and then we'll stop for a chat about it.

What might we ask?	What will we look for?	What will we learn?
What is it you have to do here? How did you know that was what you were meant to do?	Can they successfully complete the jetpack tutorial? How many times do they fail, and what causes failure?	"Do players learn how to use the jetpack"

Post task questions:
- What was that level about?
- Did it teach you how to do anything in the game? What things?
- How does the jetpack work?
- Anything confusing or difficult about the game so far?

An extract from a discussion guide. A free template for this is available on the website for my previous book *Building User Research Teams*,

BuildingUserResearchTeams.com

With the study plan created, a researcher has a lot of admin ahead to ensure the study runs as planned. Before covering that, we will look in more depth at some potential methods that might be used in a games user research study to answer research objectives.

GAMES USER RESEARCH METHODS

As described in the previous chapter, researchers need to pick an appropriate method to reliably answer their research objectives. Many of these methods aren't specific to games, but do have some nuances in the objectives or approach when applied to games that are worth describing briefly. In this chapter, we will look at some methods in turn, consider some typical research objectives that they might be applied for, and discuss some important points to consider when applying these methods to research studies.

When designing a study, it's usual that a variety of methods will be combined to get complete results. For example, understanding what players are thinking via interviews while observing their behaviour in the game, or combining observation with a survey to answer all of the research questions. Combining methods is very common when designing studies.

When working as a games user researcher, do keep in mind that only researchers are particularly interested in the method used to get results and focusing on research methods can distract when promoting research to new teams. Over time it can be useful to expose teams to the nuances of research methods to raise their literacy with research and help them identify when they could be running more studies. Early on in a relationship with a new team, you should focus on getting good-quality results, rather than the details of how the results were obtained.

Methods for understanding what players are doing

Some of the most common studies are focused on understanding a player's behaviour in the game, and whether that matches what the designer wants players to experience. This includes usability testing which identifies where players don't understand what they are meant to do (although this is a failing of the game's ability to communicate, not the player's fault).

Observation

Observation describes watching players play the game and looking out for parts where the player doesn't do what the designer expected them to do. This is a very common format for studies and is typically combined with other methods to understand why the player acted in the way they did. Understanding not just what players did, but they did it is essential information for designers to fix issues.

Probing questions are usually asked while observing, to get players to reveal their understanding of what they believe is happening and uncover gaps between how they think it works, and how it actually works. Part of a researcher's skillset is how to ask those questions without revealing information to the player - broad questions like 'what are your goals?', and 'how did you discover what you are meant to do?' are best for probing understanding. These phrasings avoid artificially altering the player's understanding of how the game works. Similarly, combining observation sessions with interviews can give another opportunity to explore a player's understanding of how the game works (their **mental model** of the game), and identify how this differs from how the designer wanted it to be experienced.

Another way researchers may decide to uncover a player's understanding is by asking them to think aloud. This involves asking players to talk about their thoughts as they play, which can reveal their understanding of the game without needing to be asked questions.

Talking aloud while playing is an unnatural task, and introduces some cognitive load, which might artificially impact a player's performance. Talking about what they are doing out loud may lead people to the right answer, which wouldn't have happened if they were playing silently at home. Another impact can be that talking out loud will distract players and create issues that wouldn't occur if they were paying attention. Because of these problems, care needs to be taken when deciding to use this method. Thinking aloud shouldn't be dismissed entirely though - sometimes this can achieve this naturally, without artificially changing player behaviour. Cooperative games are an example of this, which require players to communicate and explain how things work to one another and will reveal the participant's understanding in a realistic way.

Using observation as a research method can introduce challenges unique to games. Unlike many other types of software, games might require multiple players to play simultaneously. This can be required when testing multiplayer games, or when trying to test long sections of gameplay with multiple participants simultaneously to save time. A researcher will find it difficult to reliably observe more than one or two participants at a time and so may work with other user researchers (or train up some students) to cover these tests reliably. Study designs with multiple simultaneous players will also rely on surveys and analytics to gather data, as will be covered shortly.

Biometrics can also help support observational studies. This describes using sensors to measure responses from player's bodies as they play - for example, sensors to detect when participants are alert, or eye trackers that record where participants are looking. These tools can help focus the researchers' attention to the most interesting parts of the session, and may one day be able to do more than this and draw meaning from player's body responses. Although this has potential, many research teams don't regularly apply these methods because they increase analysis time and disrupt the player's experience without providing enough additional insights to justify the time cost. They are currently not widely applied in games development because of this.

Some typical objectives which a researcher may decide to use observation to answer include:

- Do players learn the game's objectives?

- Do players know where to go on level 2?

- Do players understand how to use fast-travel?

- Does the tutorial teach players how to use their jetpack correctly?

Accessibility testing

There are ethical and legal reasons why it's important to ensure that no-one is prevented from playing games due to disabilities, and user researchers can run studies that help make this possible.

The most effective method of uncovering accessibility issues is running usability testing with people who have disabilities, to identify parts where the game doesn't support their needs. However, usability testing can be logistically challenging to recruit for and run - many players rely on custom setups that are difficult to recreate in a usability lab. Additionally, the need for fresh participants to uncover new issues means that any participants who live close enough to visit for running studies will only be useful for a single study before their behaviour will become biased by their participation in previous studies. For pragmatic reasons researchers often supplement usability testing with other methods of uncovering accessibility issues, including using panels of users who have access needs, or reviewing against best practice guidelines.

The top research objective that accessibility testing will help answer is:

- Does the game support people who have disabilities which impact how they play games?

Analytics

Analytics describes methods that measure player behaviour. This can be achieved manually - with a researcher or the participant marking whenever an event occurs - or automatically with the game itself tracking events. Measurements are easy to compare, and so can be a simple way of comparing what players are doing to the designer's intentions - are players failing more often than the designer wants, or does one team have an unfair advantage in a multiplayer game.

Lo-fi methods of measurement, where the researcher is counting events such as player deaths, or where they fail tasks, is a reasonably common research method. In studies where multiple participants are playing simultaneously, it's not possible to closely observe behaviour and probe appropriately to understand it. As a consequence, these studies often rely on counting events, combined with surveys to determine whether players are experiencing it as intended.

Recording in-game events automatically using analytics is a specialist role, and becomes increasingly important later in development and after the launch of a game. As a user researcher, it's unlikely that you will be required to implement and measure these events yourself, however working closely with a data scientist can be a very beneficial relationship. Identifying which research objectives are appropriate for a data scientist to address and working with them to ensure that the measured results can be explained with insight from research can be a compelling argument for evidence-based decision making in games development.

Some of the objectives that analytics can help address are based around balance and difficulty:

- Can players complete the puzzle in the right time?

- Is the difficulty of the game correct?

- Is the multiplayer fair and balanced for both teams?

- Are any of the weapons overpowered?

Methods for understanding what players think

A very common research objective that teams suggest is 'do people like my game?'. Although it's not the only ingredient for success, a fun game is more likely to be successful. As a research question, this can be very difficult to answer, and might not be particularly easy to uncover or interpret.

As a first step, identifying usability issues using the behavioural methods described above can be most impactful. Usability issues will increase friction and frustrate players, reducing their enjoyment.

There is a tendency to attempt to use scores from players as a predictor of a game's Metacritic rating (Metacritic is a website which aggregates scores from review sites to give one overall score). Metacritic scores are important to many studios - some base financial bonuses on getting a high Metacritic score. Although asking players to rate their experience playing the game can give some information that can be benchmarked against data gathered in similar methods, it's very different from the ratings that would be given by professional critics. This is not only because a critic is different from an average player, but also because a player is rating the whole experience of being paid to visit a studio to play unreleased games, not just the game itself.

Beyond that, a combination of qualitative and quantitative methods can be used to uncover what people think about a game, why they think that, and how representative those opinions are. There are methodological challenges with interpreting what players think and turning it into useful information to inform game design. When caution is used to avoid teams drawing unsafe conclusions from these studies, this can be another valuable service for user researchers to offer.

Interviews

Interviews involve asking players questions, either during or after gameplay, to understand their thoughts. As covered above, observing or measuring player behaviour will reveal a lot of information about what players are doing. However, this isn't necessarily enough by itself to make decisions about how to change player behaviour. A designer would need to know why players did what they did, in order to make the right change to the game that will change player behaviour.

To achieve this, it's common to ask questions during user research studies to reveal what players think and how they understand the game to work. There may be a gap between what they understand, and what the designer wants them to understand, and so designers will try to reduce this gap by making changes to the game.

As described previously, asking questions can change a player's understanding, potentially revealing information they didn't previously have or causing them to think about the game in a manner they wouldn't have normally. Researchers learn to time and phrase their questions appropriately to cause the minimum disruption to the player's natural experience.

It's also important to remember the difference between a player's statements and the truth. This is not just people intentionally lying, but also players are subject to a number of unconscious biases which can mean their own opinion or beliefs about why they did something might not reflect what really occurred. This is most risky when asking players to predict future behaviour. Questions such as 'will you buy this game?' do not correlate well with the behaviour of buying the game, and so can be extremely misleading and unhelpful. Care should be taken with interpreting interview data, and a researcher will create the most value by analysing player's statements and focusing on the insight into the thought processes they reveal.

Some research objectives interviews might help answer include:

- How do players think the special ability works

- Why did players not go down the correct path?

- Why do players think they enjoy or not enjoy the game?

Surveys

A common research method is to use surveys to measure players sentiment around a game, or individual levels. This often takes the form of scales and ratings - asking players to rate a level out of ten, or rate the game using scales such as 'I understood what to do' or, 'I understood where to go.'

To what extent would you agree with each statement:

'I always knew **where to go** on this level'

Strongly Disagree	Disagree	Neither Agree Nor Disagree	Agree	Strongly Agree
1	2	3	4	5

'I always knew **what to do** on this level'

Strongly Disagree	Disagree	Neither Agree Nor Disagree	Agree	Strongly Agree
1	2	3	4	5

Agreement scales are one type of questions that can be used to compare levels

By itself, the figures from surveys aren't very helpful - it's meaningless to report that a game is 'seven out of ten' because this doesn't give enough information for a designer to know what to do to improve the rating. The data from surveys is most useful when compared to other results - e.g. comparing ratings between levels to identify dips, or comparing to scores of other games. It should also be combined with qualitative methods to explain why levels received these scores and what changes might improve them.

To get sensible results from a survey will usually require a lot of participants. This can be challenging for secretive or unannounced games since many studios will prefer to run those within their building where access to recording devices or the internet can be monitored. This is one reason that the multi-seat playtests can be common in games since this allows surveys to be run on-site to answer research objectives.

As a researcher, it's important to understand enough about statistics to identify safe and unsafe conclusions from the data received. One of the most common statistical tests a user researcher performs is to calculate the confidence intervals between different results, to see if there is a significant difference in the ratings between two things -

such as the ratings for each level. Many qualitative research studies will not achieve statistically significant differences between ratings, and being able to test this will help build trust in research conclusions.

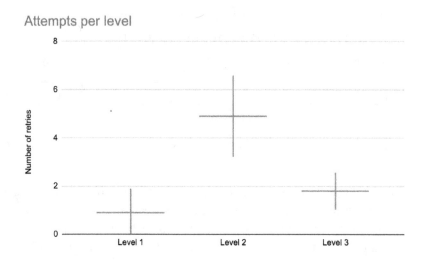

Calculating confidence intervals will be required to draw reliable conclusions. The vertical bars show the top and bottom limits of where the true value really lies.

The types of research objectives that might be answered with surveys are largely focused around player's perceptions. They include:

- Do players think this level is too hard?

- What are player's favourite weapons?

- How does the jump feel?

- Do players like the chase sequence?

Methods without users

Not all user research methods require users. Over time, user researchers develop a degree of expertise in anticipating the impact of design decisions on players. This expertise can be used to evaluate games without watching players.

There is a risk with relying on methods that don't use users. When sharing the findings from other studies, there is an objective truth in the findings - players really didn't see where to go, or players really didn't understand how to use the jetpack. This is (hopefully) indisputable- although defensive teams might start to question the quality of the participants or the study design. Because of this objective truth, when issues are identified the development team should take them seriously.

When relying on methods that don't test real users, it is easier to challenge the finding. 'Players might find it hard to use the jetpack' is less convincing than 'Players did find it hard to use the jetpack.' To get teams to take action requires the team to trust their researcher, and the researcher to not betray that trust. Being neutral and objective, and avoiding pushing their own idea or agenda is even more essential for researchers running these kinds of studies.

Expert reviews and Heuristics

One method that researchers employ is to provide feedback on issues they anticipate players will encounter, based on their own experience playing the game. Because researchers have watched lots of people play games, they are more likely to be able to correctly anticipate issues than other members of the team who may have unrealistic expectations of real player's abilities or thoughts.

Expert reviews are cheaper and quicker to run than other research methods because they don't require the time or expense of recruiting participants. An expert review can be particularly useful before running other research studies. Identifying issues that would probably occur during a study with users, and then resolving them before the study starts will allow new and more interesting issues to emerge, and will become easier as experience with running studies grows.

Despite a common title for this method being expert review, calling it that won't endear you to your team, who are experts themselves. Usability review is a less controversial title that still describes reviewing the game to identify usability issues.

Related to expert reviews is the idea of heuristics and heuristic reviews. Heuristics describe principles for good design, the most famous being Jakob Nielsen's 10 Usability Heuristics for User Interface Design[6], although game specific ones exist also. Some expert reviews will decide to evaluate against these heuristics, and refer to specific heuristics when explaining why issues exist.

Personally, this is not the approach I advocate. I believe that referring to heuristics can limit the range of issues that a researcher is looking out for. Also, many game-specific heuristics describe design decisions rather than identifying gaps between the intended experience and the experience players actually receive. I don't believe making design decisions should be part of what a user researcher does. However it is not uncommon for this to be done, and researchers should at least be aware of relevant heuristics while they are playing through the game and identifying potential issues.

Some of the more common objectives that a researcher might use an expert review to identify include:

- What usability issues do we anticipate players will encounter on this level?

- Do we believe that players will learn how to use the jetpack from this tutorial?

- Is it clear where to go on this level?

---

[6] Jakob Nielsen. 1994. 10 Usability Heuristics for User Interface Design. [ONLINE] Available at: https://www.nngroup.com/articles/ten-usability-heuristics/. [Accessed 28 October 2020]

Post mortems

When a game is complete, new sources of information become available to help understand how players experienced it. Unlike many other mediums games attract an enormous amount of attention from critics, fans and commentators which can give some insight into the quality of the experience.

Post mortems involve analysing feedback from these sources, and identifying some themes in the issues that are described. These issues can be then analysed, to understand which decisions caused them to occur, ultimately improving the game development process. This can be very valuable feedback to help consciously change how a game team works and promote evidence-based decision making.

There are some risks to be aware of when interpreting post-launch feedback for a game. Most importantly the people who give this feedback are not typical of normal players - critics are professional players trying to describe the game to a less professional audience, commenters are likely to be more extreme around their viewpoints than people who don't comment, and streamers are entertainers trying to find amusing topics to focus their videos around. This context can make their experience significantly different to that of someone playing at home, and care should be taken when applying insights learned from these audiences to more typical groups of players.

Waiting until reviews are published means it is often too late to make significant changes to that game. Despite this, running post-mortems on released games can give some information that will help improve decision making for the future. This can also be done with competitor's games, and can be referred to as a competitor analysis.

Some objectives that might be addressed with this method include:

- Did people like the combat?

- Did people understand the story?

- What are some successful ways that other games have implemented crafting?

More on Games User Research methods

Although we've briefly described some common methods here, each of these require expertise and practise to apply correctly and to safely interpret the results from. The book *Games User Research*[7] has some essays from experienced researchers that go into these methods in more depth to help a researcher apply these appropriately.

---

[7] Drachen, A., Mirza-Babaei, P. and Nacke,L., 2018. Games User Research.: Oxford University Press

PREPARING A GAMES USER RESEARCH STUDY

Preparation before running a study will ensure the sessions run smoothly and successfully answer the research objectives. The preparation needed to run a games user research study is very similar to most types of user research study - with perhaps more complexity in the technical setup and code screening required, as we will see.

Having earlier covered designing a study, in this section we'll cover all of the main stages required to prepare for running the study, and highlight some of the challenges specific to researching video games. This includes:

- Finding research participants
- Understanding the game and the build
- The technology
- The space
- The paperwork
- Preparing the game team
- Piloting

Recruiting games research participants

Most research methods need users to take part in the study. This requires finding the type of people who would play the game once it's released, inviting them to take part in the study, and then making sure they turn up.

This takes a lot of coordination and time, and it is sensible to start recruitment as soon as the study plan is complete. At this point, it will be clear how many users are needed and the session length. The amount of time recruitment takes varies based on the method used but can be between a few days and a few weeks.

We previously covered how to run kick-off meetings. In this meeting agree who the participants of the study should be, this will prevent arguments later about the participants not being representative or suitable. Recruitment should be aligned with who the game is aimed at, and can be informed by data from other teams, such as the marketing department. Some sensible criteria to recruit on include:

- Experience with other games (e.g. This is a high budget first person shooter, so we're looking for people who have played other big FPS releases from last year).

- Familiarity with previous games in the series (e.g. This is a sequel to a popular sports franchise, so we're looking for people who played the last edition).

- Demographic information, to some extent - for example if it's aimed at children. Recruiting based on age and gender amongst adults is not recommended because it risks reinforcing inaccurate stereotypes about who games are for, and furthers representation issues.

It's important to spend time making sure that the study is looking for the right kind of players. Getting the wrong kind of players means that the study's findings won't be relevant to the real game design decisions being made. If a participant has never used dual-stick controls before they will have a bad time in a study looking at a first person shooter which assumes prior experience with those controls. This may be useful when designing tutorials, but isn't relevant when testing other parts of the game, since the audience is meant to be experienced first person shooter players.

Screening participants

To make sure that the participants are appropriate, it's necessary to screen them before inviting them to take part in the study. Screening is the process of checking that they match the correct criteria for participation in that study. It's reasonably common for people to sign up to take part in studies they are not suitable for, because of the money offered to take part, so checking they are suitable is essential to avoid mis-recruits. This can often take multiple stages:

- A questionnaire asking for information about what games they play, or checking other screening criteria, written so it's not obvious which answer is the correct one to take part in the study. This questionnaire can also check their availability for the intended dates and times of the study.

- Some teams also phone participants prior to confirming their session. This conversation covers more in-depth questions to check they really have played the games they say they have.

Having checked they are the right kind of person to take part in a study, people can then be booked in to the time and dates needed for the study.

Making sure people turn up

No-shows, when a participant fails to turn up, are expensive and embarrassing. Expensive because it wastes the time of the researcher and the designers or producers observing. Embarrassing, because everyone then has nothing to do, and are sat in an observation room twiddling their thumbs until the next session is scheduled to begin. To reduce the risk of people not turning up, there are three tactics to consider using.

Firstly participants should be incentivised - given money, or something close to money such as vouchers, to pay them for taking part. This makes people more likely to bother to turn up, rather than deciding they can't be bothered on the day. It also helps find more 'normal' users - people who will do it for free are likely to be either much bigger fans, or much more vocal critics, than an average player. Recruiting only unpaid participants will introduce a sampling bias in the kind of users taking part in your research sessions.

Secondly, consider recruiting one or more spare participants. This means booking one more participant than the study requires - either to wait around all day, or as an extra session at the end of the day. If people do fail to show up, the spare can be used to make up for the missing participant.

Send confirmed participants a calendar invite and phone them the day before to remind them the study is taking place, and the time and place it will occur. This will help avoid the session being accidentally forgotten, or misunderstandings about when and where they are meant to go.

Finding the right participants takes a lot of work and is a specialist skill. Many research teams either have a dedicated team member hired to handle this or outsource it to an external participant recruitment company. Recruiting participants is complex, and perhaps the most suitable thing to outsource if budget is available to do so.

Understand the game and the build

Identifying usability and experiential issues within a game requires understanding the game very well. This not only covers understanding the intention of the game - how it's meant to work - but also the state of the build when it will be tested. This is sometimes called code screening.

Running studies prior to the game being finished will mean that the version being tested is incomplete. Also, because games are complex systems, it is very likely that there will be bugs within the version being tested. Often game teams will want to create a custom release (build) for the test. When preparing the study, researchers need to play this test version of the game enough to understand what it's contents are, what the bugs are in it, and how to overcome any bugs or incomplete sections so that this can be handled while moderating a session.

It's also sensible to check the test build against the study's objectives - is the required content in there that allows the objectives to be answered? If not it'll require a negotiation with colleagues to decide whether to change the test objectives or provide an updated build.

As well as understanding the version being tested, researchers also need to understand the goal of the game and the design intent behind it (hopefully the designers have thought about it!). The study design will require some observations to be made during the sessions (for example, where players get lost, or how many times they die). For each of these, understanding the design intent is necessary to help decide whether an issue exists. This can require a lot of conversations with the people who designed these features or scenarios to help uncover how they want the player to experience them, such as how many times they want players to fail before solving a puzzle. It also might require designers to articulate and quantify their design intent, which they might not be particularly experienced with. Building close relationships with colleagues is once again particularly important to running successful studies.

Time spent understanding the game, and the design decisions that have gone into it, will help a researcher run a successful analysis of the data that comes out of a study. This allows them to reliably identify the most important issues for the team. This preparation will also help researchers lead more useful discussions around fixing issues, informed by an understanding of what has occurred before, which will be explained later in this book.

Preparing the technology

Testing video games will inevitably require being comfortable with technology - perhaps more so than in other domains of software development. In addition to preparing the version of the game being tested, there is also technical setup required to record or stream what happens in the study.

How to prepare the build will depend on the hardware being used for testing - such as whether it's a console, mobile or PC game. Regardless of the specific process, a researcher will need to install the build and test that it is working appropriately. Because the software is still in development and hasn't gone through QA, there is a reasonable chance that technical problems will occur when installing the game into the test environment. Leave plenty of time to trial and troubleshoot this.

There is a tradeoff that will need to be negotiated with the game team - often they will want to provide the final build as late as possible so they can continue to make changes, but the researcher will want enough time to install it and check that it works as intended. Giving a deadline for the final build to be provided two days before testing starts can be a good compromise, giving the researcher enough time to react to problems.

A research study also requires some custom technology to allow the session to be observed or recorded. Many research teams have permanent spaces (research labs) that allow them to do this without having to set up the recording technology each time. Smaller research teams might have to put up with using a meeting room for running their studies. A second room will also be useful to set up an observation room - a dedicated space to encourage teams to view live. Offering live viewing increases colleagues' engagement and understanding of what's occurring in the sessions, and amplifies the impact of the studies. If a dedicated room isn't possible, many tech setups allow the sessions to be streamed live to people's desks.

Technical setups for recording video from the sessions that combine what happens in the game, with video and audio recorded in the room can be done reasonably cheaply, using a combination of screen sharing software, HDMI splitters and recording software. There are many guides online about how to build a user research lab that supports recording and streaming video for testing one participant at a time, and I covered some potential setups in my previous book *Building User Research Teams.*

A difference between games user research and other industries is the need to host many players playing simultaneously, to support some of the methods explained previously. This greatly increases the technical complexity, and some advanced lab setups that support these studies have been covered by Seb Long in the *Games User Research* book, and at the *#GamesUR Summit*, the videos from which are available on YouTube on the GRUX SIG channel.

Preparing the space

As well as setting up the room to handle the technical requirements for running the study, it's also important to think about the impact of the room on the participant's experience, and the areas the participant moves through to reach that room. The room itself should be neutral and avoid intimidating or biasing the participant. Avoid an overly clinical aesthetic that makes people feel they are being watched in a laboratory, and avoid heavy brand marketing that may change people's opinions about what they are playing.

Ensuring that the participant's experience is considered and curated throughout their interactions with the study will help create a more comfortable and natural environment. This might include giving them specific information about what to do on arrival, thinking about where they get taken when they arrive, and briefing any reception staff so that they handle the participants appropriately.

In addition to preparing the room that the participants will be in during a study, the space for observation should also be prepared. If the technical setup supports live streaming, it's often sensible to book a space where observers can view it communally. This encourages discussion between members of the development team and allows members of the research team to sit in and help guide that discussion. Preparing this space can involve ensuring that the video stream can be seen by all using a projector or large screen, creating space where post-its can be captured, and providing refreshments to encourage attendance. Booking meeting rooms can often be difficult in busy offices, so try and reserve them with plenty of time in advance.

Preparing the paperwork

Running user research studies generates a lot of paperwork, and it's easy to forget to make and print these in the lead up to a study. These documents can include:

- Pre-study information to be given to participants

- Information to be given to the building's reception desk.

- Non-disclosure agreements for participants

- Consent forms for participants

- Any surveys or questionnaires to be distributed to participants

- A method to capture the notes during the study

Templates for many of these are available for free on the website for my previous book, *Building User Research Teams* - www.BuildingUserResearchTeams.com, but we'll explain each briefly now.

BUILDING USER RESEARCH TEAMS
How to create UX research teams that deliver impactful insights.

About The Book   Free User Research Templates   'Embedding User Research' Newsletter   The Author   Get The Book

USER RESEARCH TEMPLATES

Templates for the user research process can be a great head start for a new team, allowing them to adapt the contents to meet the needs of their organisation.

Details on how to use all of these templates are in the book *Building User Research Teams*. Please feel free to download and adapt these templates for your own use.

On this page, you will find:

- The Research Study Tracker
- A Research Study Checklist
- Kick Off Meeting Template
- Study Plan and Discussion Guide Template
- Consent Form Template
- Visitor Information Template
- Observer Information Template
- Note Taking Template
- User Research Report Template

A variety of research templates are available on the *Building User Research Teams* website

Pre-study information for participants should be emailed in advance, and tell them when and where the study will occur, as well as other logistical information such as travel options, parking or what to do when they arrive. As discussed previously, no-shows can be both expensive and embarrassing for a researcher, and by making sure participants have the information to hand, and know what to expect, it will help reduce the chance of this happening.

When participants arrive at the front-desk of the building, ensuring they have a positive experience will help reduce their anxiety and encourage more natural behaviour. It's reasonably intimidating to go to a big corporate office, and making sure that any reception staff understand who they are and how to handle their arrival will make the experience less scary. To help with this, create a document for reception staff that describes who will be arriving and what actions to take on their arrival - who to call, and where to ask the participant to wait.

As covered in the first section of this book, secrecy is considered very important for many games with extensive marketing strategies. Create a non-disclosure agreement in collaboration with a legal team, and ask participants to sign it. This will help discourage leaks, and increase the studio's confidence that running user research studies is safe.

Running ethical user research requires the participants to understand what the study is about, what information will be gathered, and how their data will be stored and used. This is often handled by combining an in-person briefing from the moderator with a document that the participant can read, sign, and keep a copy of. Giving this information on a document with a verbal briefing helps ensure that the participant has understood and is giving informed consent - an essential ethical requirement. Prepare a document that explains the high-level goal of the study (without revealing too many details that may impact their behaviour), for example *"We are interested in learning about your experience with the game to help improve it"*. The document should also list the data that will be captured - e.g. audio recordings, video recordings, their survey responses. The document should also give instructions for how they can request a copy of their data or remove consent at a later point.

There are two types of questionnaire that might be useful to prepare for a study, and these can be done on paper or on a computer using survey tools such as Qualtrics. Although the participants should have been screened before they were invited to participate, it can be useful to reconfirm their habits around what games they play at the start of a session. This can help identify mis-recruits where the wrong person has been invited, participants have lied, or someone other than the invited person has turned up. It can also make it simpler to use the data about their playing habits as part of the analysis, since they will have consented to that data being collected and used on the consent form. Questionnaires will also need to be prepared and distributed when the study design requires surveys either during gameplay (for example after every level), or at the end of the session.

The last thing to prepare is the method of note-taking that will be used by any researchers working on the study. For structured studies, where the things being observed are all identifiable in advance, some teams like to use a spreadsheet for note-taking. For more unstructured studies, where the player has greater autonomy over what they do it's not possible to anticipate in advance what feedback will be collected. In these situations mind maps can greatly speed up data collection and analysis. Some details on how to do this are also covered in my previous book, *Building User Research Teams*.

Also don't forget to print out all of the above paperwork, and the discussion guide created in the previous section, before the study starts!

Preparing the game team

When running user research, it is important to ensure that the game team feels involved with the study. Their active participation increases the likelihood that the research study will impact their decision making, and justify the investment in running studies. As covered earlier, active engagement with the team to decide the research objectives, and working together to make sure the researcher understands the design intent is essential to running a useful study and interpreting the data correctly.

One of the easiest ways to fail to get buy-in is by not involving them in the study being run. At the minimum, user researchers should be inviting them to view research sessions, and invite them to a debrief where the results are discussed. Sending these invites can be easily forgotten, and people have very full calendars, so invites should be sent early in study preparation. Immediately before the study, remind the game team that the study is occurring, what the objectives are, and how they can observe the sessions will help increase engagement.

With a more mature team and an experienced researcher, once a relationship has been established and their understanding of research has improved, more exciting collaborations can be explored - such as collaboratively analysing the data from a study to come up with the results together.

Run a pilot test

Plenty of things can and do go wrong when running a study. These could include:

- The build crashes and players lose their saved game

- Bugs occur in the game that make progress impossible

- The recording device fails to record

- The microphone wasn't on, and the interview doesn't get picked up

- The consent forms weren't printed out

- The survey has the wrong scale on it

- The task set to participants was misunderstood, and people played the wrong part of the game.

In order to reduce the chance that these issues disrupt the real study, it's very important to run a pilot study. This is a practise run of the study, using a pretend participant (usually a colleague), pretending they are a real participant and running through the complete study. It's tempting to skip bits during a pilot - e.g. not asking the fake participant to fill out the consent form, or playing less of the game than a real participant would. That can be necessary when time is short, but each skipped part increases the risk of not noticing a problem with the study until it's too late.

Running the pilot the day before the study is due to begin means that the real test build can be used, avoiding the risk of bugs emerging between the pilot and the real test. The day before still gives enough time to react to most technical or study design issues that might emerge.

More on 'Preparing a Games User Research Study'.

In this section, we've touched on a lot of the tasks that a researcher will be doing to prepare to run a successful study. We've only scratched the surface, and there is a lot more work that can be done to describe and optimise these processes, as well as other considerations such as the secure handling of personal data.

The processes required for running user research studies are covered in more depth in my previous book *Building User Research Teams*, which might be a helpful resource when establishing research at a games studio that hasn't done it before.

RUNNING A GAMES USER RESEARCH STUDY

A games user research session is not significantly different from other user research sessions. The overall structure is likely very similar, and could include:

- Introducing the study to the participant

- Screening and interviewing the participant

- Performing some tasks

- Interviewing the participant

- Wrapping up the study

Although the specific contents of each step will be different based on the objectives and method of each study, there are some common themes when working with games that are worth covering.

This section will briefly describe each part of a user research study, and introduce some of the things games user researchers should be considering as they follow their study plan and execute the study.

The start of the session

As described in the previous section, when a participant arrives at the building, both they and the front-desk should be briefed on what happens when they arrive - typically waiting somewhere out of the way to be collected by the researcher. Many studios also ask the participant to lock away any recording devices at this point - such as mobile phones - to reduce the potential for leaks.

When collecting the participant, remember that this isn't a typical experience for them and they may be feeling more concerned or cautious than normal - so be kind!

The study plan created previously contains prompts for the information that should be delivered to the participants at the start of a session, which can include:

- Introducing who you are

- Explaining what data will be collected during the study, how it will be stored, and asking participants to give consent for their data to be collected and processed.

- Explaining the non-disclosure agreement and asking participants to sign it.

Be aware of local laws around consent and the use of personal data. Although this is more lax in North America than in Europe, we still have an ethical duty to ensure that participants know what data is being collected, how it will be used, and how they can remove consent. The standards required by Europe's General Data Protection Regulation (GDPR) are a good start for ethical research.

This is also an appropriate time to explain the non-disclosure agreement (NDA). Introduce what an NDA is, and check with participants that they understand they are agreeing to not talk about what they see or do in this session. Keeping secrets requires a degree of trust with participants - one way of achieving this is to describe to participants why it's important to keep what they see secret and how that allows us to continue to run studies to improve the game by running sessions that gather their feedback. Ask participants to sign the NDA, and provide them with a copy.

Having gathered appropriate consent, a researcher should introduce the study to ensure that the participant understands what is required. This can include:

- Outlining what will happen in the session, and giving participants the chance to ask any questions.

- Explaining your relationship to the game - if you didn't make it, tell the participant so and that they can give honest (and brutal) feedback without hurting your feelings.

- Explain that you're not testing them, you are testing the game and that they should say if anything seems more or less difficult than they would expect

- Explaining think-aloud (as described in the methods section earlier), if the study requires participants to talk out loud about their experience.

Templates for a standard version of this introduction are available for free on the website www.BuildingUserResearchTeams.com

What happens in the session

The specifics of a user research session will depend entirely on the study design and is difficult to generalise. Perhaps the most common types of study a games user researcher will run are one to one usability sessions, and multi-seat playtests which rely on some observation supplemented by surveys to understand player behaviour and sentiment.

For many study designs, the researcher will want to start with some questions for the participant, either asked verbally or through a questionnaire, to check that they are the right kind of participant for this study. These could ask about their typical playing habits - how much they play, what they play. This allows the researcher to put findings about their behaviour into context.

Most study designs will be asking participants to perform the tasks described in the study design. These tasks can often be very broad, such as 'play the game as you normally would at home.'. For more nuanced tasks you might want to give the participant a printed prompt that describes the task in case they forget (and ask them to verbally read it out to you to check they have understood it).

Some tasks can have success or fail criteria - such as 'Upgrade your jetpack.' With these tasks, ask players to tell you when they believe they have completed it. This avoids accidentally confirming when it's been done correctly, or that it hasn't yet been completed yet through your moderation. Also when creating tasks, remember to avoid giving away information the player doesn't already have - 'Use the pause menu to upgrade your jetpack' tells the player which menu allows them to upgrade their jetpack, and would fail to uncover if that was a usability issue.

It's common for research sessions to then end with an interview to probe the participant's understanding and thoughts about what they did in the game. This gives the researcher an opportunity to see if misunderstandings remain about how the game works, which points towards further usability issues.

Moderating sessions

Many study designs require a researcher to moderate the session - interacting with the participant directly to ask questions or hand out tasks. This takes practice to achieve the right balance between being open and friendly, without influencing the participant's natural behaviour or thoughts.

Moderators need to be neutral throughout the session. They should avoid introducing new ideas into the discussion that haven't been raised by the participant, and avoid confirming or dismissing the participant's opinions. It's critical that the moderator doesn't introduce their own opinions - this will put social pressure on the participant to change their opinion or not share their true thoughts openly. Failing to be neutral will not only bias the data being captured from the participant, but also reduce the game team's trust in the researcher's objectivity and the quality of their conclusions - reducing the impact that research studies will have.

However, a moderator cannot just sit in silence for the session, they have to actively engage with the participant to confirm and explain what is being observed. Because researchers cannot see into participants' brains, it's not possible to tell why players are behaving in the way they are, and it can be dangerous to assume. A player might head the wrong way, but without asking questions it's impossible to tell whether this was intentional or not, and why they did it - essential information for designers deciding whether to fix an issue, and how to do so. This means that researchers have to confirm and supplement their observations with information from the player on why they acted that way.

To achieve this, moderation requires an arsenal of bland probing questions which elicit information without giving anything away. These can include...

- 'What are you up to currently in the game?'

- 'What are you thinking here?'

- 'What's your goal?'

- 'How did you discover you had to do that?'

... with follow up questions to explore their response in appropriate depth, and using pauses, or repeating the participant's statements back at them, to create the opportunity for the participant to share more.

A helpful technique to ensure that a researcher is getting the required amount of information from participants is to anticipate what information the game team will need to take action. This means not just observing what the player did, but asking enough questions to understand why they did it, what the player believes is happening, and what factors within the game influenced their understanding. It also means observing what the participant did next - such as were they able to recover from the issue. Keeping in mind what a game team will need to know can help a moderator assess whether they need to probe further, or keep silent.

Another technique that moderators often use is pretending not to be an expert on how the game works. This will reduce the participant's fear of looking stupid, and also can encourage players to share their thoughts and understanding. Being humble, rather than acting like an expert who is analysing the participant, will create a friendlier atmosphere and reveal more of the participant's natural behaviour.

As covered in the method section, many user research studies involve having one moderator supervising multiple players at the same time. Although this involves less one to one interaction with participants, a lot of the same skills still apply - creating a safe space where players feel comfortable sharing their thoughts, and making appropriate interventions to ask questions where required.

Capturing data during the session

Studies generate a lot of data. Some of this is collected automatically, such as analytics generated within the game or surveys players fill out. Other data requires a researcher to capture it, including observations of player behaviour or what is said during interviews.

This note-taking task cannot be done accurately live while moderating sessions, but can be done by a second researcher, or by reviewing recordings of the session. When capturing notes, recording details of which participant this note relates to, and the time stamp for the event will make it easier to correlate notes with the recordings. Some software allows timestamps to be added automatically, or via a keyboard shortcut, and some teams create custom scripts to make this easier. Correlating the notes with the recording can be useful when the notes are incomplete, and make it simpler to create screenshots or videos to help communicate the issue.

When note-taking research sessions, it's good practice to capture everything that occurs - and save the task of deciding which notes are meaningful until analysis. Trying to note-take and evaluate the worth of each note simultaneously will lead to observations being missed which may later be relevant. It is safer to over-capture, and then make evaluating the notes a separate task as part of analysis. When capturing observations, also remember to capture what occurs after the incident being described, to help evaluate the priority of the issue. If a player gets lost and finds their way after 15 seconds, that is likely to be less important than an issue where the player is lost for 20 minutes. Capturing the resolution of each issue allows this kind of prioritisation to be done.

We've covered previously how time sensitive games development is, and there often isn't enough time to rewatch all of the sessions in full. Capturing high-quality notes first time will help ensure the results are ready faster and make it easier for the results to be ready in time to influence design decisions.

As mentioned when preparing for running a study, mind maps can speed up the process of capturing notes, in a suitable format for speedy analysis. More on this is in the previous book *Building User Research Teams*.

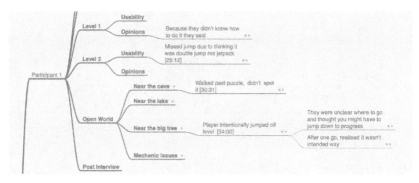

Mindmaps can speed up data capture and analysis

Wrapping up the study

After all of the tasks have been completed and any questions required by the study design have been asked, the session can wrap up. It's ethical to remind the participant of the consent covered at the beginning - what data has been captured, and what the participant can do if they want to retract consent. It's also sensible to remind them of any non-disclosure agreement they signed.

The participant will want to know about the process for getting the agreed **incentive** - are they being given cash immediately or will money be transferred to them. Explain this to them, and answer any other questions they have, while keeping within the limits of your own non-disclosure agreement.

Having run as many sessions as is required by the study design, a lot of data has been generated and it's time to start analysis.

ANALYSING A GAMES USER RESEARCH STUDY

Analysis describes the process of moving from raw data to creating some well-described findings that are useful to the game team. Well-described findings give developers enough information to take the correct action and improve how the game is experienced by players.

Game development moves very fast, and delays can reduce the impact of a research study. We want game teams to observe sessions because it increases their understanding of what occurred, and raises their faith in the findings from the study. This creates the risk that teams will start to fix what they observe immediately after the study finishes, without waiting for analysis. We believe that analysis is valuable to make sure the right action is taken from research studies, and so it would be a failure to allow action to be taken without analysis. To reduce the risk of this occurring, analysis needs to be fast and accurate. Once again, I've previously written about how mind maps can speed up analysis in the book *Building User Research Teams*.

In many studios, efficient analysis on reasonably sized studies can be done in as little as 24 hours. However, it is worth taking more time if necessary to ensure that the findings from analysis are accurate and well explained. Poor analysis will break the game team's trust and set back the cause of integrating user research into the development process.

Identify if the player's experience worked as intended

The process for analysis differs based on the study design. It typically involves reviewing the raw data captured in the study - such as the observation notes, interview transcripts and survey responses. From this the researcher will identify indicators that the player's experience differed from the experience the designer wanted them to have, and then explore the data to explain why the experience was different.

To identify where the player's experience was wrong requires an understanding of the intended design. This is why researchers need to take time to understand the game and the designer's intent prior to running a study.

Just as important is understanding and communicating where the game is working as intended. This will reduce the risk of developers making changes that break the parts of the game which players experienced as intended.

Analysis starts by reviewing all of the notes and separating all of the notes that indicate an issue, while removing observations which don't provide relevant or useful data. These can then be tagged or grouped in logical sections based on the study objectives - for example putting all of the findings about level 1 together, or putting all of the findings about combat together.

Then each grouping can be interrogated to identify the number of issues within that group. Some observations might describe the same issue - either encountered by different players, or encountered in seperate places within the game. Other observations, although on the same subject, will be separate issues. A good way of deciding if some observations are one or more issues is considering the game team receiving it - will they need to come up with separate solutions for this issue, or will one fix resolve the issue everywhere.

An example from a pretend game is these three observations:

1. Players didn't recognise where to use the jetpack in the tutorial because they didn't see the jetpack visual cue

2. Players forgot the controls for the jetpack and were unable to obtain a reminder without moderator assistance

3. Players didn't know they could use the jetpack in level 3, due to not seeing the visual indicator.

Observations 1 + 3 might be the same issue since the missed prompt was the cause of each despite occurring in different places in the game. In contrast, although observation 2 is also about the jetpack, the problem is about remembering the controls for using the jetpack, and so should become its own, separate, issue.

All of the raw data should be worked through until all of the issues are extracted.

Describing user research findings

Having identified where the player experience differs from the intended experience, further probing is required to understand and communicate why the issue occurred. Putting the work into uncovering and explaining why issues occur ensures that colleagues are able to take the right action to fix it. This is one area where a user research study will bring more value than informal playtests.

Explain why the issue occurred

An example of a poorly described issue is '*It was unclear how to complete the puzzle near the cave.*' This fails to explain why the puzzle was unclear, or what action can be taken to bring it closer to the designed experience. Because why and how the issue occurred isn't explained, the game team are unable to take the right action to resolve it.

To improve the quality of the finding, be sure to explain the cause of the issue. The cause describes what aspect of the game made the problem occur. There can be multiple causes for an issue. It may include attributes about the objects in this level ('the puzzle was the same colour as the background.') or aspects of the players experience up to this point ('previous sections had optional puzzles which didn't need to be completed for the player to proceed.').

Causes should only describe things about the game, not the player. If a cause is being written about a player ('players didn't understand...'), this is a sign that the issue isn't well understood and more investigation is needed to uncover what about the game caused players to not understand.

In this case, a better way of describing the puzzle issue would be:

It was unclear how to complete the puzzle near the cave.

- *Cause: The puzzle was grey on a concrete background and didn't stand out from the wall*

In this example, the cause clearly describes something about the puzzle which was wrong and will direct the designer towards some potential ways to fix it. Well described causes should always be transparent about why the issue occurred and describe real things. Poor causes rely on domain knowledge or are written to make the researcher look smart. *'Cause: The puzzle's appearance fails Nielsen's first heuristic and gestalt principles.'* impresses no-one and reduces the chance that the development team will take the right action to resolve the issue.

Careful moderation is needed during the sessions to ensure that the correct cause is established, and other potential reasons are identified and eliminated. As covered previously, the moderator needs to expose and test their hypotheses about why issues occur during the session rather than relying on their assumptions. Many causes are invisible without understanding what players were thinking at the time.

Explain what happened next

Describing what happened because the issue occurred is useful in order to decide how important the issue is. There is a difference in importance between issues which cause players mild inconvenience and ones that are impassable and require players to use a walkthrough to progress. Furthermore, in many games, failure is an intended part of the experience, so describing the extent of the failure is needed to decide whether the issue exists at all. To capture this, describe the impact the issue has on players. Unlike the causes, this should describe the players experience, and how this differs from the intended experience.

A version of the example issue which includes the impact could be:

It was unclear how to complete the puzzle near the cave

- *Cause: The puzzle was grey on a concrete background, and didn't stand out from the wall*

- *Impact: Players didn't spot the puzzle as the correct way to proceed and carried on exploring the cave*

- *Impact: Players didn't learn how to enter the cave and backtracked through the level for up to thirty minutes. Some needed moderator assistance to proceed.*

In this example, we've also specified how long it took players to overcome the issue, to help game teams decide whether this is the experience they want players to have. Proper preparation for the study will allow the researcher to identify and explain how each issue differs from the intended experience to help prioritise the issues in the most meaningful way for the team.

By using a standardised format, such as the cause and impact example above, it helps researchers verify that they have included all of the relevant information the game team will need, and speeds how long it takes to interpret issues.

When describing issues, researchers need to be careful to focus on the problem and avoid describing potential solutions. The reasons for this are covered in more depth in the debrief section, but in brief, their solutions can appear naive and fail to take into account what the game team has tried before or what is feasible in the production schedule. This will impact the trust a team has in a researcher's competence. One area to be particularly vigilant about is that solutions don't sneak in as causes. *'This issue was caused by the lack of a tutorial'* implies that the solution is a tutorial, and will limit the potential solutions a team might come up with.

To ensure that issues are fully described, with clear causes and impacts, it's often helpful to peer review this with other researchers who also understand the game before sharing it further. This will help protect the credibility and trust you have established with a game team.

Prioritising user research issues

For studies which identify usability issues, it's likely a lot of issues will be discovered. Resolving issues creates work for the game team, and this time commitment needs to be balanced with other development work, such as adding features or fixing bugs. Games development is often a very time-pressured environment, and so not every issue can be addressed.

Because of this, games user researchers need to rate the severity of the issues they report so that the game team can quickly decide the appropriate priority for them amongst other work.

There can be a tendency from novice researchers to over-exaggerate the impact of usability findings, rating them all as critical issues, to make their work look important. Conversely, some researchers can be tempted to under-exaggerate the findings, and rate them all low, thinking they are being nice to their team. Both of these behaviours make prioritisation difficult for producers, and damage trust with a team.

To avoid this, applying a standardised method of rating the severity of issues will reduce the chance for researchers to subjectively influence the severity. This will help game teams decide how to fit the work required to resolve issues amongst other tasks they need to do.

There are different ways of achieving this, and many studios have their own preferred in house method. A method I like is a four-point scale for issues:

- Critical
- High
- Medium
- Low

To decide the appropriate severity, I use a version of the method described in the Userfocus article 'How to prioritise usability issues'[8].

Each issue starts as 'Low'. Then ask three questions about the issue. Each time the answer is yes, raise the severity up a level.

In the context of games, these questions are:

- Is this something that the player needs to do to progress?

- Did the moderator need to step in to help resolve the issue?

- Once the player had overcome the issue, did they know how to avoid it when they encountered it again?

Some studios use 'how often did we see it in testing' as an alternative question to rate issues instead of 'did the player overcome it when they encountered it again'. Neither of these questions are perfect. If a player only encounters the potential for an issue to occur once, it's impossible to judge whether they would overcome it in the future. However, 'how often did we see it' can be an unreliable thing to count in small qualitative studies. Considering which question is more useful for the method being applied, and being consistent in applying it, is probably the best approach for rating the severity of issues.

These questions only work directly for usability issues and aren't suitable for describing behaviour. Deciding and applying severity criteria consistently is important for every kind of research finding, not just usability issues. An alternative scale will be needed for other types of finding.

Having understood, described and prioritised each issue, analysis is now complete, and it's time to share it with the team. It's common for colleagues to ask for early results before analysis is complete - for example, at the end of a day of research. Although this can be a nice opportunity for building positive relationships with colleagues,

---

[8] Userfocus. 2009. How to prioritise usability problems. [ONLINE] Available at: https://www.userfocus.co.uk/articles/prioritise.html. [Accessed 12 June 2020].

researchers should also be careful. Before analysis, it's not always clear what the true cause of the issue was, or the severity of issues, and sharing information too soon can encourage teams to start working on the wrong thing. Taking time to fully analyse the results will demonstrate the value that a researcher brings to running user research studies, and will lead to better quality games.

DEBRIEFING A STUDY

In the previous section, we covered how to identify and describe issues from a user research study. These then need to be communicated with the game team accurately so that the right action is taken to fix them. Doing this well is essential for research studies to have an impact - teams won't be able to act on findings they don't understand.

A debrief can have two stages, and it's sensible to separate them. First, they should communicate what was learned in the research study. Then, because you have gathered a lot of experts in the same room, it is also an opportunity to start to decide what to do to address the issues discovered.

Sharing what was learned

Following analysis, we should have some fully explained findings written in accessible language. Assuming the study design was appropriate for the research objectives, the findings will be relevant and address the team's current priorities.

These findings can then be communicated in a report, for example in a presentation or a word document. Presenting the findings live, rather than just sending a report, will create a better understanding of the issues for the audience. This leads me towards recommending capturing findings in a presentation, such as PowerPoint or Google Docs, supported with videos and screenshots where required.

QTE and Story Prompts can be hard to see

 Story Decisions can be hard to see

• **Cause:** The decision options have poor contrast and are difficult to see against the background

• **Cause:** The scene has a time limit, encouraging players to react quickly

• **Cause:** There is no confirmation once a selection is made

• **Impact:** Players can make important decisions without being aware of the range of choices available to them

• **Impact:** Players can unintentionally make significant decisions in their story

The two selection areas when making story decisions can be hard to see

An example of a report slide describing a usability issue

A format for this report can be:

- Remind the team of the research objectives

- Briefly cover the method & the audience for the study

- Then present each issue in turn, in order of priority

This can then transition into a structured activity on deciding what to do about the issues covered, as we'll discuss next.

When creating a presentation or document, to share with the team, keep in mind that the report will have two audiences. One is the immediate room being presented to. The second is people who the report gets forwarded too, or who come back to it in six months, when the researcher isn't around to present it. This means that the report needs enough context about what was tested, which build it was and what the tasks were that the report will make sense to an audience who wasn't there for the original debrief.

Although presenting the report is best because it gives the researcher the opportunity to take questions and explain any misunderstandings, this isn't always possible and sometimes the report is sent ahead without being presented. Because of this, it's important that the report covers all of the context for the issues within it, and explains why the issues occurred in enough detail that the development team can confidently make the right decisions to address the issues.

Deciding what to do

The point of games user research is to make games better, so teams need to make changes based on what was learned in the study. Although deciding and prioritising tasks will largely be the responsibility of a producer, a researcher can help start this process by starting the discussion and acting as a facilitator to help teams decide what to do.

The ideal format for this is one that encourages divergent thinking - coming up with a variety of ideas - then convergent thinking in order to assess which solutions are best.

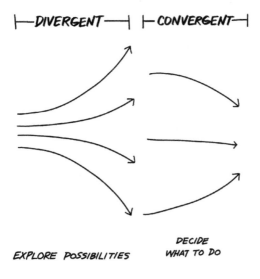

The best solution is often discovered by considering multiple options before committing to a solution.

Some researchers decide to include recommendations for actions in their report. This can be helpful when direct contact with the game team isn't possible, but it does have some risks.

Although researchers have a lot of understanding about player behaviour, this is only one aspect of the 'best' solution, and they lack a lot of other domain expertise. For example producers will understand what's feasible in the time available, artists will have better domain expertise about what is aesthetically appropriate and programmers will be able to advise on what's technically feasible. A researcher's recommendation won't understand these elements to the same depth that other disciplines do, and may come across as naive.

When a researcher gives solutions, it can also influence the ideas that follow it, reducing the breadth or creativity of ideas explored. Setting challenges instead of solutions can help prevent this. A challenge can encourage creativity, such as 'how might we ensure players know this puzzle is essential for progress?', instead of a closed recommendation 'An NPC should tell the player this is the way to continue'.

When possible, the ideal solution will take the insight from all of the disciplines and combine them. This isn't always possible, as scheduling all of the relevant leads can be challenging - one of the reasons the calendar invite for the debrief is made during the preparation for the test. If relevant colleagues are available, one way of generating recommendations is with a workshop, which can be run back to back with the debrief.

A potential structure for this workshop could be:

- Reviewing the highest priority issue

- Spending five minutes individually thinking about potential ways of addressing the top priority issue

- Sharing the ideas with the group and having a short discussion to evaluate each

- Voting on which should be explored further, incorporating elements from other ideas discussed as necessary

- Assigning it to a specific person to explore further, either the producer or a lead from a relevant discipline

- Then repeating this cycle with the next highest priority issue, until the group has run out of time, issues, or enthusiasm

As this workshop runs, the researcher can facilitate it and note the ideas discussed and the favoured options. These can be shared when emailing the research report. A researcher can also help steer the group to avoid the solutions which seem easy but aren't compatible with what we know about player behaviour. A very common example of this is trying to fix every issue with another tutorial, which players rarely read, without appropriate thought given to the context in which the tutorial will appear.

This collaborative method of deciding solutions allows all of the disciplines to input on the potential solution, will increase everyone's engagement with the findings from the study, and should lead to better quality design decisions.

Regardless of the final design decisions made, it's likely that further studies will be required to check that they do fix the issue. Design is an iterative process. As this study ends, it's sensible to start again with identifying what the most important research objectives are, and planning the next study.

WHAT ELSE DO USER RESEARCHERS DO?

Running high-quality studies is important, but it is not the only skill a games user researcher needs. For impactful studies, user researchers need to be trusted and have colleagues who are ready to accept evidence to inform their decision making.

This doesn't necessarily happen by itself, and a user researcher will also need to be an evangelist for evidence-based decision making, and educate their colleagues about the potential of research.

Earn trust

Earning your colleagues' trust is never complete. Trust atrophies over time, as new people join the studio, and as priorities change. Researchers always need to be working on improving their relationship with their team.

The key to earning trust is to do high-quality work. High-quality work includes:

- Define the scope of studies appropriately so that they are relevant to what the team needs to know.

- Avoiding introducing your own subjective opinion and basing all findings on reliable, well sourced data.

- Avoiding over reaching with the conclusions, caveating and being open about the limitations of studies.

- Delivering on time and ensuring that deadlines are met. The process for user research studies is reasonably structured and repeatable, and so there is no reason why the dates agreed in a kick-off can't be met.

- Being a nice person to work with, helping out colleagues and not being thought of as a barrier to progress. Clearly explaining why you are saying no helps with this when necessary.

Being trusted creates more opportunities for running studies and will increase the impact that researchers can have. Running studies isn't free - beyond just the financial cost of running studies, there is also the time cost of reacting to the findings, and a production cost of preparing appropriate builds - so there will be resistance. Being trusted, with colleagues invested in research will create more opportunities to run research earlier in the development process, and get time dedicated to reacting to research findings. This will make games better!

Educate colleagues

Studios often start with little experience of user research. Even those studios who are well versed with evaluative studies, such as usability testing, may be unfamiliar with running other types of studies to understand their players better and make better quality design decisions earlier.

This unfamiliarity means that some potential studies might be missed. Because the game team isn't aware where studies can help them, they might not actively seek out their researcher and ask about it. If a researcher isn't close to decision making, they will be unaware of the opportunity, and the study won't happen. This will lead to worse decisions being made.

To overcome this, active education of colleagues is needed. This can include:

- Presenting to colleagues about the types of research studies that exist, and how they can be relevant for the design decisions they make.

- Writing blog posts and sharing case studies publicly, or via internal newsletters.

- Creating internal team sites to share research reports and information on research.

- Running fun research-related activities.

- Actively talking about the studies that have been run, posting executive summaries prominently on walls and in virtual collaboration environments, such as Slack.

Proactive research propaganda can also help, as the UK's Government Digital Service have had tremendous success with. Their posters and stickers describing research and design principles have had a huge impact, such as 'Two hours every six weeks', promoting observing user research sessions, and 'Understand Context', describing the need to understand users' situation before designing for them.

Publicly posting information about user research and creating posters and stickers to push research concepts could help create a positive buzz and interest in user research studies.

GUR Poster designs by Chloe True. See them in full colour on the website.

Some posters and stickers to help promote research at games studios are available on the website www.GamesUserResearch.com

Over time, education can help change people's understanding, from research being considered a one-off activity at the end of development, to recognising the value that iterative studies throughout development can bring. Game design decisions happen throughout development, and as covered in the first section of the book, there is potential for research to help improve the quality of those decisions at every stage.

TIPS FOR NEW GAMES USER RESEARCHERS

In this section, we've covered a lot of the tasks a games user researcher does. As we've seen, being a user researcher can be hard. As well as being able to plan, run, analyse and debrief studies, they also need to work closely with a lot of other disciplines to prove the value of their work.

There are some mistakes that new user researchers sometimes make when working with other disciplines. To finish this section, I want to expose some of them, to allow a new researcher to avoid them and make new, more interesting, mistakes instead.

Be humble

Be humble. If you find yourself thinking you are smarter than your users, or your colleagues, it's likely you haven't understood the situation correctly. Users haven't had the same exposure to the development of the game that you have, and it's entirely normal that they will encounter usability issues. Colleagues are experts in what they do, and there's likely a good reason for why the obvious fix hasn't been made. Assume everyone is doing their best, and recognise that compromise is necessary. Start by understanding the constraints people are working on, and why decisions have been made, before dismissing people as ignorant or shortsighted.

This doesn't mean that you shouldn't question decisions. As a user researcher, you will have been exposed to some information about player behaviour that colleagues won't have. Make sure that you are sharing the relevant information you have, so that everyone is making fully informed design decisions. Everyone is trying to make the best game possible, so help them get the information they need to do so.

Be proactive

It takes work to get people to listen to user research findings. As covered previously, building trust is a long term project, but it is necessary to avoid research reports being put in a drawer and forgotten about. If you just send out research reports without following up with the team, half of the findings will be misunderstood and the other half will be ignored. Instead, being proactive with colleagues and pushing for research to happen, making sure colleagues understand the findings and encouraging them to retest are all parts of the job too.

Be specific

Avoid vagueness. When presenting findings, make sure that you understand why they happened, and that you have fully explained this. Don't just say something is clear or unclear, explain what it is about the implementation of it that makes it clear. I see vagueness particularly with studies describing user behaviour, such as creating personas that describe 'types' of players. A goal of 'have a fun time' isn't specific enough to be useful, and isn't exclusive enough to differentiate this persona from anyone else.

Make sure you are giving enough detail for your colleagues to make good decisions.

Be open

Do good-quality work - make sure that you can justify the conclusions made based on appropriate study designs and appropriate tasks.

We need colleagues to trust research findings are safe, and unbiased. To achieve this might also require explaining what bits of your findings are unsafe. A common example of this is game teams not understanding why what looks like a higher score for a game or level found in a study may not actually represent a significant difference - we cover more on the specifics of this in the next section of the book.

Being honest about what the limitations of a study are will help build faith in the accuracy of the findings that you do endorse. It also requires researchers to be very clear when they are presenting their own opinion, versus what is a reliable finding based on evidence.

Be a games user researcher

As we've seen in this chapter, being a games user researcher requires a combination of the ability to run research studies, being able to work well with colleagues and an understanding of how this fits into a wider games development process. A challenge for new researchers is being able to demonstrate this in order to get a job, which is what we'll cover in the last section of this book.

PART 3

STARTING A CAREER IN GAMES USER RESEARCH

Understanding how games get made and how to run research studies is required to be a games user researcher. Unfortunately, those qualities alone aren't necessarily enough to get paid to be a games user researcher. There are not many jobs out there and a lot of competition, so it can be difficult to stand out against everyone else in a tough market.

In this final section, we look at the factors that make getting a job difficult, the hiring process, and the skills to develop in order to be the best possible candidate for a games user research job.

We'll end by also considering some of the downsides of a career in the games industry, to help decide whether this is the right career for you.

By the end of this section, you will understand how to demonstrate different research skills when applying for games user research roles and how to increase your odds of getting the job.

IT'S HARD TO GET A GAMES USER RESEARCH JOB

Getting that first job in games user research can be very difficult. There are lots of people interested in joining the industry at a junior level. There are also more people doing relevant university courses than jobs exist for, and so competition is fierce.

As covered in the first section of this book, working in games sounds glamorous and exciting, and is an industry that people feel passionate about. This glamour attracts people to want to work in games, and there is a lot of interest in entry-level roles in every discipline. The skills needed to be a user researcher may seem less concrete to a layperson than 'I can programme a game' or 'I can make professional-quality art'. Because of this, some people feel confident applying for games user research roles, without necessarily understanding what the role is. This leads a large number of applicants for any entry-level user research role.

However, there are usually few candidates who have both an understanding of how to design, run and analyse user research studies, and an appropriate understanding of games in order to be able to communicate sensibly with players and other industry professionals. This means there is an opportunity for people who can demonstrate both to stand out from the pack.

Unfortunately, the large amount of competition isn't the only thing that makes it hard to get a job as a games user researcher.

There are not many games user research jobs out there. In many industries, user research is recognised as an essential part of the software development process. Unfortunately that is not yet the case in games, and many studios don't yet employ user researchers, or rely on outsourcing it late in a project's development. This means that the roles that exist are often aimed at a senior level - looking for someone who is confident being the only user researcher on a project and needs no support to do it. This will change over time as the recognition of the value of user research grows, but does create challenges for juniors looking to join the industry now, who will only have a limited number of studios to pick from.

Watch out also for job roles which claim to involve user research, but don't give appropriate time or support to do it properly. A red flag can be broad job descriptions, such as 'UX/UI & User Researcher'. Although all of these disciplines care about understanding user behaviour, being a user researcher requires different skills to being a UX designer. The broad remit of this job title means that finding time to perform each part well will be difficult and may require some conflict with bosses to run appropriate user research studies. User research is likely to particularly suffer from pressure to drop it when time is short because it's harder to measure 'we made a worse decision' than 'we didn't create some wireframes'. Adverts for these broad multidisciplinary roles may indicate that the team has low research maturity, and can be a red flag that they may not be supportive of running the high-quality studies we think are important. Because of a lack of alternatives, it's not always possible for someone joining the industry to turn down these broad roles. It's important to go in with realistic expectations of what it might be like.

Based on the number of junior roles advertised some of the larger studios such as Ubisoft, Player Research, EA, Microsoft, Sony and Activision may be good places to look at for junior roles, as well as the tech behemoths such as Amazon and Google. Also look at mobile game studios, who can have software development processes closer to app developers and may be more prepared to incorporate user research in that process than traditional game studios. Being actively engaged in the community will help identify appropriate opportunities - more information on how to be a good community member is later in the book.

Because of the small number of games user research jobs, there are a limited number of places where games user research happens. Hubs in Canada, West and East coast US, France and the South of England, are where most the roles are. It's likely that a new researcher would have to move to these areas once offered a job because remote roles are rare. For many people, this can be impossible due to other life commitments.

This has an unfortunate impact on representation in GUR. Because jobs in games user research are rare and may require people to have to move home, this creates a bias in the candidates that apply for these roles, towards younger people who have the time and financial security to be able to move for their career. This is made worse by some of the other issues we covered about games earlier, such as being prepared to give up your personal time for crunch. This excludes many people from being able to apply for or get jobs, such as people with caring responsibilities or family commitments. Over time, this is a thing that the industry should actively recognise and address with more flexible working hours, remote work and job shares, but this is not yet common.

Because of all of these challenges, it's important to have a serious think about whether this career is right for you. There are lots of other industries where you can make more money doing user research, so you should think carefully about your priorities.

If I haven't put you off applying for a job in games, read on and we'll look at how to stand out from everyone else applying for the few games user research jobs out there.

GET EXPERIENCE AS A GAMES USER RESEARCHER

Being a user researcher requires specialist skills, and it's necessary to demonstrate these throughout the hiring process to come across as the best candidate.

The most important skill is a history of successfully planning, running, analysing and debriefing user research studies. This is a catch-22 situation - to be able to get a job as a user researcher, you need to demonstrate that you can work as a user researcher, which is hard to do without having a job as a user researcher. Challenging! In this section, we'll look at some of the ways this experience can be acquired and practised.

Academic experience

It is very common for games user researchers to have completed postgraduate courses. The 2018/2019 Games User Research salary survey indicated that over 70% of people working as games user researchers have completed postgraduate education, such as a Masters or PhD[9]. Often, user researchers have graduated from programmes offering coursework in human-computer interaction, informatics, ergonomics, social psychology, psychology, sociology, anthropology, or media studies.

Doing a masters course or a PhD in the social sciences helps develop an ability to plan and run reliable studies with real participants and emphasises the need for rigour in uncovering and explaining research findings. Social scientific degrees often require conducting human-subjects research - studies which involve interacting with people to collect data (e.g., running an experiment to explore motivations to play a game after watching trailers with different sets of content).

---

[9] Games Research and User Experience Special Interest Group. 2019. Salary Survey. [ONLINE] Available at: https://grux.org/career/salary-survey/. [Accessed 12 June 2020].

Because usability testing and playtesting are human-centric research, a postgraduate education in the social sciences can be a helpful way to gain this experience before getting into the industry. This experience, and the rigour that academic research promotes, is helpful for building trust in research findings when working with a real game team and can set a candidate apart when applying for jobs.

As part of many postgraduate courses, there will be the opportunity to get experience planning and running real studies. These can become useful things to include on CVs and talking points for demonstrating these skills in a job interview. Sometimes hands on research experience can be done with external industry partners, exposing the researcher to some of the demands of working in a non-academic environment, and giving further evidence to future interviewers that this might be a suitable candidate for a job outside of academia. Not all university programmes offer experience with external industry partners, so make sure you do your research or ask the programme's graduate director about such opportunities before committing to a programme if you are keen on developing practical experience.

The time scales for academic study depend on the country. However, there are commonly two levels of postgraduate course - a shorter Masters course lasting one to two years, or a longer PhD course, lasting three to five years (or more!). Serious thought should be given to whether a PhD is appropriate for you, since it is such a long time commitment, and doesn't necessarily make you a better candidate for a job than someone who has done a Masters combined with some practical experience. Having to apply to junior and mid-level roles, despite developing years of expertise in a subject, can lead to disappointment and disillusionment for some PhDs entering the job market. There are lots of good reasons to do a PhD, most importantly passion for the research topic being worked on, but it isn't necessarily the best use of your time for a career in games user research.

For those who are ready for the commitment required, postgraduate study can be a very successful method of developing many of the skills needed to be a user researcher. However there are some differences between academia and industry that are worth noting in order to be prepared.

One limitation of academic research experience is that the time scales for research projects are different in industry. As covered in the previous section of this book, there is intense time pressure in games development, and it's not uncommon that a study may need to be planned, run and debriefed in ten to fifteen days. In academia it might take longer than that to get an ethics board to decide whether the study can be run at all. Finding other ways to demonstrate that projects can be run to tight deadlines with limited resources may be necessary during an industry interview. For instance, a masters or PhD graduate interviewing for games research jobs might instead speak to working under tight deadlines to submit a paper or how they developed project management skills while leading a team of researchers in an academic lab.

A second limitation is that the research questions in academic study are often explored at a very deep, often theoretical, level, and become very specialised. This level of depth is often not appropriate for industry, where the research objectives will often be simpler, such as *'Can people complete this level?'* Finding the right balance between pragmatism, rigour and getting useful results on time will be a cultural change required moving from academic to industry. A PhD graduate will have to become comfortable with conducting less theory-driven work and recognise that sometimes the research methods in industry are aiming to just be good enough for informing the game team.

Another difference is the need to make their language accessible and direct. Academia has a reputation for using complex words and dense writing to demonstrate expertise in a subject. This will be a barrier to game teams understanding the point researchers are making and reduce the impact of research studies. Clear language, with short simple sentences, is essential for working in industry. Aim to be direct and to the point.

With an awareness of these differences and the extra work involved, academia can be a great place to develop the skills needed to run human-centric research studies and will generate great examples to reference in job interviews.

Get a different user research job

The most direct way to demonstrate that you can work as a games user researcher is by getting a job as a user researcher in another industry. Working in an in-house or agency research team will require defining briefs, planning studies, running studies and debriefing them, which will be fantastic evidence for any GUR job. For interviewers, this experience will create confidence that the candidate can be a researcher in a commercial environment.

There are some differences between user research in games and user research elsewhere, as covered earlier in the book. One is the type of research objectives that might exist - efficiency and time on task might be more relevant in other software, but is not relevant when designing entertainment experiences like games. There are also some methodological differences due to the different types of research objectives. Anecdotally, I also notice a difference in rigour between games user research and the conversations I see user researchers in other industries have. Amongst games user researchers, accuracy and verifiable evidence for findings seems to be the core point of the job (as it should be to build trust). Outside of games, weak evidence signals seem to go unchallenged more frequently, and more discussions focus on how research creates empathy for users rather than evidence of behaviour. This is just my anecdotal experience, and may not be the case everywhere. Regardless it's still good advice to not be sloppy with the evidence for your findings when talking to games user researchers.

Understanding these differences, and also separately developing an understanding of games, how they are made, and being able to reference aspects from popular titles, would make a very strong candidate for any games user research role.

This isn't necessarily an easy path - it's hard to get a junior user research role in any industry. Being open to taking a job in another sector then transitioning later with more experience opens up additional opportunities to someone interested in becoming a games user researcher.

Get a different job in games

In the past, a popular way into any games role was to start in Quality Assurance (QA). As covered early in the book, some junior QA roles can be an entry-level role in games, looking for bugs by playing and replaying builds endlessly.

A decade ago, this was a sensible way to learn about the games industry, and transition into other roles, such as design or user research. In fact, some fantastic user researchers started in QA. However, I would no longer recommend this as a reliable way of getting employment as a games user researcher.

Working in QA doesn't help develop or demonstrate skills around planning and running studies. Due to the increased recognition of the field of games user research, and relevant academic courses, there are a growing number of people who have research experience, either from their degree or from working in user research in other fields. This means that they are likely to be much more suitable candidates for a junior user research job than someone working in QA.

It isn't impossible to get into a games user research job from QA - it will expose some of the process of creating games, which is a helpful context to have. Some smaller teams might also have less distinction between roles, and someone ambitious working in QA can also push to run usability or user experience studies. This is rare though, and it's likely a hiring manager will find it easier to teach a researcher about games development than teaching a game developer about running good research. Because of this, standing out as a competitive candidate with only a QA background can be difficult.

Personal projects

Some of the skills needed to be a user researcher can be demonstrated through personal projects - planning and running studies independently.

This can be done in collaboration with independent development communities, found on popular forums like Reddit. By spending time talking to an indie developer to understand their current priorities, then offering to run an expert review to identify usability issues, a researcher can practise a lot of the client and research skills that will be relevant for a paid user research role.

Research skills can also be practised when playing released games by identifying usability issues. However, the experience from this is less relevant - the games are usually polished and the researcher has no insight into the constraints that the game team were under and which compromises were made. This can lead to reviews which fail to take into account the real pressures of the game development process, and can appear overly negative. Working closely with a mentor who is familiar with some of these constraints can help.

A limitation with getting experience through personal projects is that it lacks the opportunity for peer review - there is no feedback from experienced researchers who can help identify problems with the research being done. Combining this with mentoring can help fill that gap - the IGDA's Games User Research and User Experience mentoring scheme can be found at grux.org. Personal projects also encourage working for free, so they should only be run with hobbyist developers rather than devaluing industry research.

It is difficult to recommend that everyone does personal projects. Having the freedom to spend personal time running research projects is a luxury that many don't have, and can exacerbate current representation issues in the industry. Some of the prompts in the next section of this book describe discrete tasks that can be done to practise research skills over long periods of time, and may be more accessible. Unfortunately, it is still more difficult for people with care or other responsibilities to dedicate free time to personal projects.

We cover more about how to demonstrate appropriate research skills in the next chapter of this book.

Which is the right approach?

As covered, competition for user research roles can be tough. We've discussed getting experience from academia, other research jobs, other games jobs and personal projects. The unfortunate thing is that other people going for roles will likely have experience from more than one of these sources, making it hard to stand out.

That doesn't mean that any of these are essential - there are many well-respected games user researchers who don't have relevant academic experience, or for whom games user research was their first research job. Because the competition does have a lot of experience, it's really important to make sure you are practising and demonstrating the right skills to stand out from others.

SHOWING THE SKILLS NEEDED TO GET THE JOB

The application process for games user research jobs can be long. It's not rare for hiring to include any or all of the following steps:

- Looking at a CV or resume

- A questionnaire about gaming habits

- Interviews with user researchers and people who work with user researchers

- Moderating a user research session

- Performing an expert review

- Presenting some research findings

Not all hiring processes will involve every one of the above steps, but as roles become more senior, hiring managers may start to expect more of them.

Each of these tasks have a different objective of what they are trying to assess. We'll cover what those goals are before going in depth on how to demonstrate relevant skills for each.

The CV review is verifying that the person applying for the role is a vaguely sensible candidate. Because video games are a prestige industry, every role gets lots of applicants who just want to work in games, rather than having a specific desire to be a user researcher. Since being a user researcher requires specialist skills, it's unlikely that someone with no history or interest in research would be an appropriate candidate. So the CV review will primarily be looking to make sure that this person is a sensible candidate for a research role and has any kind of relevant academic or personal experience that indicates they are not just applying to every games job they see.

A questionnaire, or call with a recruiter, can sometimes be used to assess whether the candidate plays video games ('What games have you played recently?') and would be able to talk confidently about them. Some may ask people to identify usability issues with the game, to verify that the candidate can recognise the difference between a usability issue (where the implementation of a feature fails to meet the design intent), and the candidate's subjective opinion (something they do or don't like about the experience).

Interviews are always part of the hiring process. They explore the candidate's experience with research, and ask for examples where they have previously run studies. Because past behaviour is the best predictor of future behaviour, these examples will be used to assess the candidate's decision-making process. For example, exploring how the candidate has previously matched research objectives to methods, how they have decided the appropriate method to use to share findings with an audience, or how they have handled situations when they have had multiple demands on their time. With these questions, the hiring manager can assess whether the candidate is making conscious and purposeful decisions. It also allows the candidate's communication skills to be assessed - can they clearly explain their view and justify their decisions?

A moderation task involves the candidate being asked to run a user research session, observing issues and interviewing a participant as if it is a real study. This will probably be combined with tasks before-hand to create a study plan, run the session, and then a feedback session where the candidate can share some things they observed during the session. This will, of course, be limited because it's not a full study with enough sessions for in-depth analysis. This task will help evaluate the candidate's ability to moderate a session appropriately, asking sensible non-leading questions, putting the participant at ease and allowing appropriate usability issues to be identified.

Another method of evaluating research skills that is reasonably common is asking candidates to perform an expert review. As described earlier in the book, an expert review asks the candidate to play a section of a game and identify usability issues. They will then likely produce a report or presentation to be shared with the hiring manager. This will test the candidate's ability to identify appropriate issues and communicate them.

Other ways of assessing research skills could include asking the candidate to develop a research plan for a hypothetical testing scenario or evaluate a set of survey questions for any potential issues.

A moderation task or expert review is often combined with a presentation task, where the research findings will be presented to an audience - either of researchers, or of other game development professionals. This will give further insight into the candidate's ability to communicate issues comprehensively and accurately. This presentation task is often done with an audience of developers who are not researchers, in order to most closely recreate the audience for a real study and make sure that the candidate is able to communicate well with other disciplines.

Although no hiring process will involve all of these stages (hopefully), the same skills will be explored. These include:

- Client Skills

- Study design

- Moderation

- Analysis

- Presenting

- Facilitating skills

- Understanding the sector

We'll explore each of these in turn, to make explicit how recruiters will be looking for these criteria.

Client Skills

Being a user researcher involves interacting with other colleagues who don't have the same background or experience. This includes meetings and discussions with designers, developers, producers, artists and others to understand what questions they have that a research study might be able to answer.

Communication is obviously very important in these interactions - ensuring that everyone has understood the same point, and that consensus has been reached about how to proceed. A researcher needs to ensure that everyone agrees on the research objectives and the approach that's been chosen to answer them. Client skills become more important as a researcher's seniority increases and the impact of their research grows.

When applying for roles, being able to demonstrate a history of working with other disciplines and helping them understand what research is, or how it applies to their work, will be essential for being a successful candidate.

To demonstrate this, think about opportunities when you have had to work with people from different backgrounds - such as group projects, working in multidisciplinary teams, or presenting research findings to non-researchers.

Some activities to consider for practising these skills:

- Visit the Reddit *'r/playtesters'* forum and look at the request for playtests. Read some requests, and consider what kind of feedback they are asking for. Think about how to articulate these as research objectives.

- Imagine you have been asked why recruiting representative participants is better than using people off the street. Consider your reasons why, and explain it in terms non-researchers can understand.

- Write a blog post aimed at non-researchers to explain some of the benefits of running user research studies early in development

Study Design

Once research objectives are agreed, and everyone knows what they want to learn from a study, the next stage is to be able to match the objectives to an appropriate method. This includes deciding how the research objectives will be answered (is it a questionnaire? Is it observation? Is it eyetracking?) and what the prompts or questions will be - what task will be set to the participant, or what will you ask them, to reliably answer each of the objectives within it?

Showing the ability to pick sensible methods and tasks, and demonstrate that they are appropriate to the research objectives, will be essential. This may be challenged during the interview process to make sure that the decisions were considered and made with conscious intent.

To demonstrate this, explain the factors that were considered when deciding research methods. This will likely include identifying the 'correct' method, and then describing any compromises that had to be made for pragmatic reasons such as time or budget. Demonstrating thoughtful consideration of complicated and sometimes conflicting factors will be part of what the hiring manager is looking for

Some activities to consider for practising these skills:

- Take the following list of research objectives, and decide an appropriate method to answer each. Justify why.

  o Do players like my game?

  o Why are players leaving my free-to-play game after two weeks?

  o Is my game too difficult?

  o Does my tutorial work?

  o Do players know how to solve the puzzle on level 2?

- Consider a game you have recently played. Write a study design that discovers whether a new player can successfully learn how to use the core features.

- Imagine you have been challenged by a team member on why a playtest with five users is appropriate. Consider what objectives it would be appropriate for, which it wouldn't and why.

Moderation

Being a user researcher means a lot of direct contact with members of the public - the users being researched. Some hiring processes will want to assess this, and check that the applicant can be friendly and open with users, put them at ease, and get them through a study, without falling into any traps such as leading their answers, or failing to uncover why the behaviour observed is occurring.

To demonstrate this any experience of having run usability or user research sessions and being exposed to users first hand will be good evidence of appropriate moderation skills.

Some activities to consider for practising these skills:

- Think about what questions a participant will have before they arrive to participate in user research. Write an email that prepares participants appropriately to take part in a study.

- For a game you have played recently, decide what previous experience a potential participant should have to take part in a study on that game. Decide what questions you would ask to uncover whether someone had that experience.

- Observe a friend play a game they haven't played before. Ask them questions to understand what they are doing and thinking, while minimising the amount you change their behaviour.

Analysis

Having run a session, the next part of a user researcher's job is to identify sensible findings from the raw data. This will involve identifying which of the things that occurred during the session are meaningful and interesting, which are not appropriate to share, and extracting them. Analysis also involves making sure that the issues are explained comprehensively and understood in enough detail that a designer can take action based on it. The cause/impact structure discussed earlier in the book can help with this.

This experience could often be gained in an academic setting, from running experiments or studies, and reporting what was learned from them. As covered previously, industry or personal projects can also create evidence for this.

Some activities to consider for practising these skills:

- Play a game you are unfamiliar with, and list the issues you encounter. Categorise each as to whether it's an opinion about the game, or a usability issue

- Pick one of the usability issues you identified, and think about what questions you would ask the designer to understand how they intend that part of the game to work.

- Think about a usability issue you have encountered in a game recently. Write it down in a way that someone who has played the game but didn't see the issue would understand. Describe what caused the issue to occur, and what the impact of the issue on players would be.

Presenting

One of the most common ways of sharing findings with a development team is with a presentation - such as the report covered earlier in this book. This requires the confidence to stand in front of people, and clarity in communication to make sure the issues are understood. Once again, the audience for these presentations are usually non-researchers, and so using accessible language is important.

This experience of presenting in front of audiences doesn't have to come from a user research role, and other examples of presenting can be ways of demonstrating this, such as project work or presenting in any industry.

Some activities to consider for practising these skills:

- Imagine a study that answers the research objective 'Did players like this game?'. Decide what context about the imaginary study you might want to give a game team when presenting the findings.

- Create some slides that describe usability issues you have recently encountered in a game. Make sure the issues would be understandable by someone who hasn't played the game.

- Record yourself presenting some slides on usability issues, and listen back. Assess whether you have successfully communicated the issues you encountered

Facilitating

Researchers are often called upon to run workshops, and help team members generate and evaluate solutions to the issues uncovered. Any experience of running workshops, and being confident facilitating a session with a group of colleagues, may be explored during the hiring process.

This experience can be developed through group projects when studying or working in many non-researcher job roles.

Some activities to consider for practising these skills:

- Read about divergent and convergent thinking that help generate and evaluate ideas, and search for some design workshop activities that can encourage this. Think about how this can be applied to addressing usability issues in games.

- Think about group activities you have participated in before and how you have felt taking part. Identify some things that could have improved people's confidence contributing.

Understanding the sector

Because working in games requires interacting with other people who are interested in games (both colleagues and participants), understanding popular titles and being confident talking about them is important. For example, if a participant described that the inventory system is similar to the one in *Destiny*, it's going to require knowledge of *Destiny's* inventory system to be able to understand their point and articulate it to others.

As covered earlier, games user research also has some nuances compared to other sectors, including that some difficulty is intended, and that efficiency isn't the primary goal. Being able to articulate how games user research is different to other user research disciplines may be assessed during a hiring process.

It's reasonable to assume during a hiring process that a studio will ask about your experience with their own games, so be sure to play them beforehand.

It isn't essential for researchers at a junior or mid-level to have experience working in games before, however an understanding of the industry and how games work will be expected. As covered in the first part of this book, this will allow a researcher to be able to identify appropriate times to run research studies, sensible objectives and inform good design decisions.

Some activities to consider for practising these skills:

- Visit some online game development forums, and look at what topics developers discuss. Consider why these topics are important for their discipline.

- Interview a game developer to understand what decisions they have to make in their job. Think about how user research studies might make those decisions easier.

Other skills

There are some complementary skills that are not essential for a user researcher, but can help show differentiation in a competitive job market.

Should researchers learn stats?

The first is knowledge of statistics. Although it's not always expected for a researcher to be an expert on quantitative data analysis, and deep data analysis tasks will often fall under the responsibility of other teams, some basic understanding will be useful for many common research tasks.

This includes being able to identify when research objectives should be answered using quantitative methods rather than qualitative research - most commonly when something needs to be measured, such as difficulty or ratings.

A common statistical technique that researchers will be asked to apply is identifying if the difference between two results is statistically significant. This can be useful when comparing the scores that players give - for example their rating of the difficulty of two levels, or the number of deaths that occur for each team in a multiplayer game. There are calculators online that allow this to be done automatically. However, by understanding the calculations being done, a researcher can help spot errors and draw sensible conclusions from the results.

Having a basic understanding of statistics will also help avoid errors, such as knowing the difference between mean, medium, mode as well as nominal, ordinal, and discrete data. A very common mistake is averaging ordinal data, such as the scales used in some surveys. This is very frequently done in industry, including by myself, but isn't as correct as representing the responses in buckets on a bar chart. Being aware of some common statistical techniques will help reduce errors, and increase other colleague's confidence in the quality of research findings.

In many teams there will be the opportunity to do a lot more with statistics, particularly with smaller teams who don't have dedicated data analysts. In any environment, these basics will help run high-quality research and make it easier to work with other colleagues with statistical expertise.

Should researchers learn to code?

In addition to statistical knowledge, a common question in many disciplines is 'should I learn to code?'. For a researcher, it is by no means essential to learn how to code, although some do.

There are some opportunities for this to be a useful skill for a researcher. The research process requires some manual tasks, such as data analysis or report creating which can be automated with scripts, and being able to programme will make optimising those processes easier.

It has some secondary benefits - such as increasing the researcher's knowledge of what's not possible when considering potential solutions to identified issues, but time spent understanding other disciplines, such as design, will be just as beneficial.

Ultimately programming is unlikely to be one of the assessment criteria that a studio will use, and so I'd hesitate to recommend spending time learning it to become a games user researcher. Using that time to practise core research skills would be more sensible.

CVS, PORTFOLIOS AND CASE STUDIES

When applying for jobs, it's very likely that the hiring manager will want to see a CV or resume. It's less likely, but not impossible, that they will ask for a portfolio.

For a games user research CV, a lot of general advice for any CV is still relevant, such as putting the most relevant experience first and avoiding typos which will be interpreted as a lack of attention to detail.

The hiring manager will be looking for evidence of planning, running and debriefing studies and of working with people from other disciplines. Bullet points can make finding this experience easier for hiring managers. For each role, the examples should be specific, for example:

- Designed and ran fifteen qualitative and quantitative user research sessions for *game* using methodologies such as observation, surveys, interviews and metrics.

- Recruited participants using a variety of methods including external recruiters, guerilla testing with staff, and research participant mailing lists.

- Analysed and reported issues to clients with presentations and running stakeholder workshops. Ensured that the findings were incorporated into the game development backlog.

- Performed expert usability and accessibility reviews throughout development. Identified *number of* issues which were resolved prior to launch.

This can be combined with a more general skills section, which lists not just the methodologies that you are comfortable with, but also experience with the process around running research and working with clients. Combining this list with specific examples in the role descriptions will make a stronger CV. An example of the items in this skills section could be:

- Usability testing (moderated, unmoderated, lab-based and remote)

- Survey creation and analysis

- Expert evaluation

- Contextual research

- Data analysis including affinity mapping and prioritisation

- Presenting and workshop facilitation

- Creation of reports, personas, journey maps, and information architecture

- Participant recruitment

Other elements to put in the CV include any relevant academic experience, publications or articles.

A lot of user research work isn't very visual, and so many hiring managers won't ask for portfolios. Some that do may be confusing researcher with a more design-focused role, or misunderstanding what UX is. However, preparing some case studies showing how research questions were gathered, investigated and answered can be a beneficial exercise in order to prepare for interviews and to work out a narrative for describing your previous experience.

For a user researcher, if you decide to create a portfolio, it should be a collection of a few research studies, focusing on the process, the decisions the researcher made, and the impact that these studies had. A portfolio is judged on the worst piece of work within it, so fewer high-quality case studies will be better than including a lot of work that doesn't reflect well on the researcher.

A suitable format for a case study would be to include:

- What was the situation with the game and the team, including their history with research studies

- How did you identify the most appropriate research objectives to answer

- How did you decide an appropriate study to answer those objectives

- What were the constraints that the study was under

- What the study was

- What were some of the things learned in the study, how were these communicated and what impact did that have on the game.

In all of these steps, it is not just important to describe what work was done, but also why you made the decisions you did. Hiring managers will be looking to understand how sometimes conflicting demands were managed, and how accuracy was balanced with pragmatism. Ultimately impact is what user researchers are trying to achieve, so demonstrate the steps taken to achieve that.

Due to the importance of secrecy in games, this can be difficult to do while under non-disclosure agreement, and it's entirely possible that a researcher won't be able to make a portfolio based on released games. Even if it's not shared, the exercise of thinking through the above for your projects will help create strong answers to interview questions. Combining this with some personal projects from indie or evaluations of released games that are not under an NDA will also be strong evidence for a hiring manager to assess.

When creating portfolios or case studies, remember that the reader is likely to be busy and reading many similar portfolios. This makes clarity of communication the most important thing to aim for, rather than flashy visuals - this isn't a visual design role.
Clear structure is key.

A (fictional) example case study

Usability Test for UX Assault

The situation

The student puzzle game UX Assault was looking for feedback on their vertical slice before entering full production. They had run some informal playtests, but not worked with a user researcher before. I approached them and offered to give structured usability feedback to improve the quality of their game and help prioritise work done during production.

Defining research objectives

Through interviewing the lead developer, and through reviewing the questionnaire they had sent to playtesters, I identified the priority research objectives that would be useful to the development team before production. These were:

Research Objectives

Do players learn all of the mechanics from the tutorial?

- Combat
- Healing
- Crafting
- Climbing
- Using the minimap

Is it clear where to go in level one?

Do players discover how to defeat the boss?

What are players perceptions of the difficulty?

The research objectives agreed with the lead developer

From this I created a kick-off document to get consensus on the objectives and started to plan the study.

The study

To answer these objectives, I decided to run some informal one to one usability tests with representative players. This allowed me to pay attention to each participant individually and observe usability issues they wouldn't self-report. Because no budget was available, we were unable to pay to recruit enough participants to reach saturation, and so I supplemented ad-hoc tests with an expert evaluation.

Study Plan: UX Assault

Research Objectives

- Do players learn all of the mechanics from the tutorial?
  - Combat
  - Healing
  - Crafting
  - Climbing
  - Using the minimap
- Is it clear where to go in level one?
- Do players discover how to defeat the boss?
- What are player's perceptions of the difficulty?

Study Plan

Introduction

- **Welcome:** Hi, my name is Joey Joe Joe. Today we will be looking at a new game, but before that there are some things I need to tell you.
- **Consent:** First of all is consent for today. There is a form to sign, but before that I'll explain the key points. This form says...
  - That we will be recording the session today, including what happens on the screen and what we talk about.
  - These recordings are mainly for our note taking, in case we miss anything, but they might also be seen by other people inside our company. They will not be shown publicly to people outside the organisation, and will be deleted after <how many> years.
  - It also says that you can take a break, or leave at any time without giving us an explanation.
  - It also explains that you can request for the information we record to be deleted. It has details on how to do this.
  - Please read through the form and ask any questions. If you're happy you can sign it.
- **The session today:** So today, we'll be looking at a new game. This will involve us having a brief chat about games. Then you'll play for a bit, and I will ask you to look at certain bits. Then we'll have a final chat to round up at the end.
- **I didn't make it:** I should let you know that I didn't make the things we'll be looking at today. The reason I mention that is you should feel free being honest about what you like and don't like. I won't take it personally.
- **We're not testing you:** There's no right or wrong answers today, and we're not testing how good you are at using computers or this game. If anything seems more

difficult than you'd expect, tell us and we can tell the people making it to make some changes.

- **Imagine you're doing this at home:** Mostly we'd like you to use this as you normally would at home. If you do get so stuck you would give up at home, let us know and we'll help out.
- **Any questions:** Do you have any questions about anything I've covered so far, or what we'll be doing today?

Pre Interview

- What games have you been playing recently?
- What do you think about (game they played?)
    - Anything you particularly like about it?
    - Anything you don't like?
- Have you ever heard of a game called 'UX Invaders'?
    - What have you heard about it

First Task - Tutorial

Task: Imagine you have just downloaded this game, and are playing it for the first time. Please play this tutorial level, and then we'll stop for a chat about it.

What might we ask?	What will we look for?	What will we learn?
What is it you have to do here? How did you know that was what you were meant to do?	Can they successfully complete the tutorial? How many times do they fail, and what causes failure?	Do players learn all of the mechanics from the tutorial? • Combat • Healing • Crafting • Climbing • Using the minimap

Post task questions:
- What was that level about?
- Did it teach you how to do anything in the game? What things?
    - How does the combat work?
    - How does healing work?
    - How does crafting work?
    - How does climbing work?
    - How does the map work?
- Anything confusing or difficult about the game so far?

I created a study guide to lead the sessions

I moderated the sessions and recorded what occurred, which I documented later. Using affinity sorting, I identified all of the usability issues observed and prioritised them based on understanding the design intent gained from my interview with the developer. From this I created a report which I presented to the development team. The report was created in a powerpoint format that would work as a presentation, but also be understandable as a stand alone document.

The impact

This study identified 15 usability issues, including four critical issues. Left unresolved these issues would have created significant barriers for players and prevented many from completing the level.

An example usability issue uncovered in this study

After presenting the report, the team incorporated all of the issues into their backlog and will address this during production. I have booked in a follow up to help assess the fixes with further testing.

A CAREER IN GAMES USER RESEARCH

Early in the book, we covered why working in games can be hard. Before dedicating time to studying and becoming a games user researcher, it's sensible to understand some of the downsides of working in the industry. This will allow you to make an informed decision about whether games user research is the right career for you.

Because working in games can be prestigious, fun and interesting, there are a lot of people who want to do it. This has a negative impact on salaries, and pay is less within games than in other tech companies. The 2019 Games User Research salary survey indicated that a researcher with five years experience in the UK earns £45,000 on average[10]. In contrast, a salary survey in the same year by Zebra People found that user researchers with equivalent experience working in finance in the UK earn between £50,000 and £80,000[11]. Direct comparison is dangerous because the methodologies used to gather the data are different. However, it does imply that there is a difference in salary between sectors, and that games is a lower paying sector for user researcher roles.

This isn't just the case for user researchers, it's the same across the whole games industry - most people could be making more money working on other software. This does have some upsides - people working in games are there because they want to be, which is positive. Unfortunately, a lower salary will have an impact on your lifestyle, which can be particularly difficult for people with families.

Because there are fewer user research roles than in other industries, working in games will also limit where you can live. Unfortunately,

---

[10] Games Research and User Experience Special Interest Group. 2019. Salary Survey. [ONLINE] Available at: https://grux.org/career/salary-survey/. [Accessed 12 June 2020].

[11] Zebra People. 2019. Salary Survey. [ONLINE] Available at: https://zebrapeople.com/resource/digital-salary-survey/. [Accessed 12 June 2020].

game development often happens in more expensive cities. Again, that is fine for many younger people, but over time can also be detrimental to family life. The lack of roles may also impact progression, and it may be more challenging to find increasingly senior roles as your career develops than in other sectors.

Crunch, as covered in the first part of this book, also becomes a bigger issue over time. When you are young and childless getting home at 2am, or sleeping in the office can be fine. This becomes impossible if you have care responsibilities and can have serious impacts on people's personal lives. This pushes people out of games.

It would also be unrealistic to not talk about the toxicity of some of the game industry's fanbase. Although most developers are very lovely and inclusive people, incidents such as gamergate highlighted that misogyny and sexism still exists in games. Some people who identify as gamers will be hostile towards women working in games. Although this problem exists in a lot of technology jobs, it is probably worse in games than elsewhere due to many of the most vocal fans being young and lacking appropriate life experience to understand the impact of their behaviour. This can be very difficult for women working in the industry who can be subjected to a lack of respect from both colleagues and gamers, and a risk that their lives can be massively disrupted by internet trolls. This is important to consider when thinking about a career in games.

The impact of these downsides is a high turnover of staff in the industry with many people leaving as they encounter these issues. A survey from the Games Developer Conference reported that the majority of people working in games have worked in the industry for less than ten years, indicating that people move out as their career develops[12].

To put all of this in perspective, it's worth remembering that getting a job in games now doesn't mean you have to work there forever.

---

[12] Ismail, R. (2020) 26 January. Available at https://twitter.com/tha_rami/status/1221483278814863362 (Accessed: 12 June 2020).

Working as a games user researcher does develop applicable skills to move into many other user research roles. However, care does need to be taken to avoid stunting a career. Compared to some other industries, the maturity of research in games is low. This means it can be rare to get the opportunity to run contextual and **generative** research to understand people's behaviour in the real world and inform design decisions, rather than just testing things that have already been designed. This lack of experience of generative research can make it difficult to get a senior role in other sectors which will expect that experience. While working in games, advocating for running generative research can therefore be beneficial - not just to make better decisions as part of the game development process, but also for getting relevant experience to continue your career.

As covered at the start of this book, working in games can be great, and many people have rewarding careers developing video games. I hope these issues don't put you off deciding to become a games user researcher. Understanding these issues before committing to a career in games will help prevent disappointment and disillusionment.

THE GAMES USER RESEARCH COMMUNITY

Games user research has a very active community, and a lot of fantastic people volunteer time and effort into advancing the field. This has created an open and safe environment for user researchers to share knowledge and develop, quite contrary to the secretive environment around the actual games people work on.

The International Game Developer Association Games Research and User Experience Special Interest Group (IGDA GRUX SIG) is the most prominent example of this. They run initiatives to help promote user research in games, including:

- Conferences in North America and Europe

- A mentoring scheme

- A Discord server with chat channels for asking questions or sharing work, and a reading club for UX articles

- A website with links to jobs, articles, and presentations

This is not the only expression of community in games user research. Another prominent example is the @gamesUR Twitter account which shares articles about research, as well as many academic conferences looking at advances in games user research.

Being an active member of this community helps with your own personal development, by exposing you to other researchers, their challenges, and giving a space to ask questions safely. It can also create new opportunities. Being an active member of the community, and contributing to their initiatives can create a positive reputation. It's said that 70% of jobs never get advertised. I don't know if that is true in games, but non-obtrusive networking can help give an edge in interviews, and taking part in community initiatives is a method of networking that doesn't come across as creepy.

In all user research roles, I would also advise maintaining a LinkedIn profile. Recruiters are very common in tech jobs, and as you become more senior, this will also expose more job opportunities.

Being an active member of the games user research community isn't possible for everyone, as some people have other commitments that prevent them from dedicating time outside of work. When possible, it is a great opportunity for personal development while helping advance the field of games user research. Everyone was new once, and sharing your own experiences of being new to the industry will help others going through the same in the future.

THE END: LEVEL UP

In this book, we've learned what it is like to work in games development, what being a games user researcher involves, and some tips for developing a career in GUR.

As we've seen, being a games user researcher can be difficult. Getting that first job is hard because the competition is fierce. Staying in games can be equally difficult and require career or personal sacrifices to stick with it.

We've also seen that games can be a very rewarding career, with the opportunity to work with passionate people on products people love. That alignment between passion and work is rare, and shouldn't be dismissed. Both during my time at PlayStation, and on projects since, I have found games hold some of the most interesting and rewarding research challenges.

The medium of games is always changing, especially as industry interest in subscriptions and game passes rises, and the first time player experience becomes even more important for player retention, and a game's success. This will mean plenty of interesting and impactful research studies, and I'm excited to see how a new generation of games user researchers tackle these challenges

After finishing this book, as a next step, I'd strongly recommend picking up the book *Games User Research* by Anders Drachen, Pejman Mirza-Babaei and Lennart E. Nacke. The book goes into depth on each research method that we've touched upon and includes some great case studies about them being put into use.

Joining in with the IGDA Games Research and User Experience SIG Discord is also highly recommended, to discover community initiatives and professional development opportunities. This can be found on the IGDA GRUX SIG website www.grux.org

Further resources to help you start your career in games user research are also available on this book's website www.GamesUserResearch.com

I have wanted my message throughout this book to be that user research makes games better. You now have no excuse. Let's get started.

GAMES USER RESEARCH GLOSSARY

Game development and user research both often use complex terms. That's not great, as it can be a barrier to being understood - which will reduce the impact of our work.

In this book, I've tried to avoid overly technical terms, and have hopefully explained complicated terms where they have been unavoidable. In addition, I've decided to include this glossary which explains many of the words used for games development and user research - in case I've failed to explain elsewhere!

AAA - Triple A refers to the high profile, big budget games. Some famous examples include *Grand Theft Auto*, or *The Last of Us*. There are a variety of opinions about what specifically the A's refer to (An 'A' rating for factors such as budget, marketing, studio size or development time come up), but the sentiment is that this is a blockbuster game created by a large studio.

Augmented Reality (AR) - Games which overlay video content on the real world - for example taking a video stream from a camera and showing an image which adds virtual characters. *Pokemon Go* is a popular example of this, which uses the mobile phone camera to make it look as if Pokemon are in your local park.

Build - A version of the game created during development. Game makers separately work on each aspect of the game using their own tools - such as creating the levels or programming enemy behaviour. A build compiles all of the separate streams into one playable version. Studios do this regularly throughout development, and a user researcher will often have a bespoke build made for them to run a study on.

Crunch - A period of intense development where longer working hours, or working over weekends is required to meet a deadline. Crunch is covered in more depth in the first section of this book.

Designer - In the broadest sense, a designer is anyone on the team who makes decisions which impact the final game that emerges. This includes producers deciding which features to prioritise, artists deciding how characters should look, and narrative designers deciding what should happen in the story. Some details on specific design roles are covered in the first part of this book.

Design Intent - Designers have a vision about how they want the game to work, or how they want the player to feel. Sometimes this is defined and written down, sometimes it's just thoughts in their heads. User researchers need to understand the designer's vision for each aspect of the game to evaluate whether it is working as intended.

Discussion Guide - Also known as a 'Study Plan'. This document describes what happens in a user research session, and is used by the moderator during a study to ensure that it runs as planned - especially helpful if there are going to be multiple moderators working on the same study. How to create a discussion guide is covered in the middle section of this book.

Evaluative Research - Some research studies test to make sure that the design works in the way the designer intended. This helps teams actually deliver the experience to players they want to deliver. Usability testing is a common example of this. More details on different research methods are covered in part two of this book.

Features - Features describe the things in the game that the player does which differentiate it from other games ('this game features weapon crafting.'). The word feature is often used interchangeably with **mechanic**, but some would describe the feature as the outcome of a group of mechanics.

Findings - Each research study learns lots of things ('Players don't know how to complete the cave puzzle'). Every individual 'thing' that is learned in a study is a finding. They are discovered by looking at groups of observations or interview data, and include the information on why this behaviour or event occurred. The middle part of this book covers how to analyse research data to generate findings.

Games as a service (GaaS) - Games which have continual updates providing new content. Often they can be funded by subscriptions, or by offering additional items for players to purchase. *Fortnite* is a prominent example.

Generative Research - Also sometimes called 'formative research' or 'discovery research'. Some research studies learn about player behaviour beyond just playing the game being worked on. Understanding what players already know or do can help inspire design ideas, or improve the implementation of different features. Research methods are covered in more detail in part two of this book.

Incentive - It's normal in research studies to pay people to participate. This can be in money, or in vouchers. It's best not to offer merchandise, or nothing, since then only people who are enthusiastic about the game will agree to take part, which will skew the results.

IP - Intellectual Property. In games this is used to refer to a series, or character, although the term really describes legal ownership over a concept or series. This can include licensed characters (like *Spiderman*) and video game exclusive series (like *God of War*).

Kick-Off Document - A document which captures the details of an upcoming round of research, including the objectives, dates, types of user and method proposed. Running a kick-off meeting is covered in the middle section of this book.

Loop - The gameplay loop is the activities that the player actually does in the game. For example in *Minecraft* the player has to collect resources to build shelter, build shelter to survive, and survive to collect more resources. In many other games players kill monsters to earn money, which allows them to buy better equipment to kill more monsters. Many games can be broken down to a few core repetitive activities.

Mechanics - Mechanics are the building blocks of features, although the terms are often used interchangeably. The example feature 'the game features weapon crafting' covers many mechanics - an inventory, collecting items, discarding items, combining items to create weapons, selling weapons. Each of these mechanics will be designed, and requires players to understand how they work to successfully implement the feature.

Mental Model - An understanding of how something works. Players form a mental model of how each aspect of the game works, based on cues such as what it looks like and what reactions the game gives them to their actions. Designers also have a mental model of how each aspect of the game works. Successful teaching often relies on ensuring that the player's mental model matches the designer's understanding of how their game works.

Observation - Many research methods rely on watching people play and noticing where their behaviour isn't what the designer expected. Watching players is called observation. More details on research methods that involve observation are covered in part two of this book.

Participant - The players who take part in research studies are referred to as research participants. The middle section of this book covers recruiting participants.

Research Objectives - Also referred to as 'research questions'. These are the goals of the study, describing what that study intends to learn. They are different to the actual questions that participants get asked. A research objective might be 'Do players know where to go?'. To answer that research objective the interview questions asked to participants may include 'where do you go now?' and, 'how did you learn which way to go?'

Study - In user research, a study is the process of running research activities (such as interviews or usability sessions) to answer research objectives.

Studies are often described with a name based around their method or objectives, such as 'Usability Study' or 'Enjoyment Study'. This can get particularly confusing, since there is not yet a consistency in how studies are referred to. Some examples of terms people may use to refer to studies include:

- *Usability studies*, which describes studies where the objectives are focused on a player's understanding or ability to perform in a game. This description is named after the study's objective.

- *Opinion testing*. This describes studies where the objectives are focused on whether players enjoy a game. Some synonyms that exist for this type of study include Experiential testing, Appeal testing or Preference testing. This description is also named after the study's objective.

- *Biometric Testing* describes studies which gather measurements from player's bodies, such as their heartbeat, to inform the conclusions drawn from the study. This is an example of a study being named after the method being used to gather data within it.

- *VR Testing* describes studies for **virtual reality** software. This is an example of the study type being named after the medium of what is being tested.

Study Plan - See **Discussion Guide.**

Usability - Usability is how 'usable' something is - how successfully can players perform the task to complete their goal. In games, this covers whether players understand what they are meant to do, and whether they can do it. This has more nuance than in other software, because games are meant to involve challenge. In games, usability issues only describe the unintentional challenges that exist, not the challenges the designer wants the player to experience. Identifying usability problems is one of the more common types of study a user researcher runs.

UI - User Interface. This describes the things that the player sees to represent the state of the game. This includes menus, button prompts, health bars, maps, highlights and other things that indicate to the player what is happening currently or what they are meant to do.

UX - User Experience. The User Experience describes the impact a game has on the player. This is created by the combination of everything about the game - the gameplay, the difficulty, the graphics, the usability, how much it costs, the controls, and more.

VR - Virtual Reality. The player wears a headset so that the game completely encompasses their vision, creating the illusion of being inside a computer-generated environment. Unlike **AR**, the game environment is entirely computer-generated, rather than superimposing computer generated images on the real world.

ACKNOWLEDGEMENTS

Thank you to Nida Ahmad, Seb Long, Jess Tompkins and James Berg for their guidance and advice on the contents of this book. I am very grateful to each of these games research and UX stars for giving up their evenings and weekends for reviewing drafts, and their contributions greatly improved the book, while helping me avoid some silly errors!

Thanks also to Chloe True for her excellent graphic design skills creating the book's cover, helping with formatting and making the excellent Games User Research posters and stickers available on the gamesuserresearch.com website.

Thanks to Dr Graham McAllister for introducing me to the world of games user research during his HCI course at Sussex University.

When I first started at PlayStation, I joined an extremely supportive research team who helped me learn what it means to be a games user researcher. Thanks to that original team - Bryn, Cyril, David, GiGi, Julien, Lauren, Lorna, Mirweis and Moh for everything they taught me. As the team grew, I was lucky to have the opportunity to work with many other excellent researchers and team members - thanks also to Amy, Charlene, Gokhan, Hatty, Luis, Mark, Miranda, Rob, Thomas and Till.

The IGDA Games Research and User Experience Special Interest Group has been a supportive community for user researchers for over a decade. Thank you to all of the steering committee for giving up their time to help encourage and guide the community. Thanks to Anders Drachen, Ashley Brown, Audrey Laurent-André, Ben Lewis-Evans, Ben Lile, Ben Weedon, Bill Fulton, David Milam, David Tisserand, Elise Lemaire, Elizabeth Zelle, Emma Varjo, Graham McAllister, Hannah Murphy, Heather Desurvire, Ian Livingston, James Berg, Janus Rau Sorensen, Jennifer Ash, Jordan Lynn, John Hopson, Kevin Keeker, Kirk Rodgers, Lanie Dixon, Laura Levy, Lennart Nacke,

Magy Seif El-Nasr, Marina Kobayashi, Mike Ambinder, Nicolaas VanMeerten and Sebastian Long.

Thanks to all of the Games Research and User Experience mentors who have given up their free time to help students learn how to become great user researchers. I am always impressed by their dedication and commitment to giving back to the community. Adam Lobel, Ahmed Ghoneim, Alexis Raushel, Alistair Greo, Andrea Abney, Audrey Laurent-André, Alistair Greo, Ben Lewis-Evans, Ben Lile, Brice Arnold, Celestia Koh, Charles Somerville, Chloe Snell, Cyril Rebetez, Daniel Aparicio, Daniel Kutz, Daniel Natapov, David Sinclair, David Tisserand (for the third time!), David Zuratzi, Elizabeth Schmidlin, Emma Varjo, Hannah Murphy, Harvey Owen, Henrik Edlund, James Berg, Jason Schklar, Jean-Luc Potte, Jess Tompkins, Jim Stanhope, Jimmy Zhou, Joe Florey, Johan Dorell, John Hopson, Jonathan Dankoff, Jordan Lynn, Jozef Kulik, Kacey Misskelley, Karl Steiner, Kevin Keeker, Kirk Rodgers, Lanie Dixon, Laura Levy, Lennart Nacke, Lucas Rizoli, Luke Fraser, Mark Friend, Matt Streit, Mike Ambinder, Moh Khan, Morgane Schreiber, Nathan Varjavand, Nicolaas VanMeerten, Pejman Mirza-Babaei, Phil Keck, Ray Kowalewski, Robert Tilford, Sarah Romoslawski, Sebastian Long, Steven Mathiesen, Surabhi Mathur, Tania Martelanc, Ula Karpińska and William Hardin.

In 2021, there has been an exciting revamp of the mentoring scheme, led by Hannah Murphy. I'm really excited to see how the programme continues to develop!

And most of all, thanks to my wonderful wife Emma for her support and guidance during the many hours producing this book. It wouldn't have been possible without her!

ABOUT THE AUTHOR

Steve Bromley is a user researcher based in London.

He was a user researcher for Sony PlayStation's european team for five years, where he worked on games such as *No Man's Sky, Horizon: Zero Dawn* and *SingStar*, and hardware including the PlayStation VR headset and the Augmented Reality experience *Wonderbook*. He continues to offer usability and user research services for video games and virtual reality.

Steve started and continues to run a Games User Research mentoring scheme, in collaboration with the IGDA GRUX-SIG community. In the last five years, the scheme has partnered over one hundred students with fifty industry professionals from top games companies such as Sony, EA, Valve, Ubisoft and Microsoft, and helped many people find their first job in games. This book covers many of the topics that mentees have asked as they start their games user research career. Steve also co-created the first industry-focused european games user research conference.

This is his second book about user research. For more on user research from Steve, and to get updates on the book, follow him on:

- Twitter: @steve_bromley

- His website: www.stevebromley.com

BY THE SAME AUTHOR

Building User Research Teams is a practical guide on how to start a new user research team from scratch.

Learn how to:

- Advocate for user research inside your organisation
- Budget for and equip a research team
- Create the templates and tools needed to run research
- Run studies that are impactful and accurate
- Optimise your research team's workflow
- Grow a research team long-term

Available as paperback and ebook, find the book on Amazon or at BuildingUserResearchTeams.com

TAKE THE NEXT STEP

Ready to continue your games user research journey?

Join the mailing list at gamesuserresearch.com for:
- Entry level user research jobs
- Deep dives on research methods
- Stories and guidance on moving from academia into industry
- Tips for transition experience from other sectors into gaming
- Networking opportunities
- Opportunities for professional level feedback on portfolios, CVs, resumes and interview techniques

gamesuserresearch.com

www.ingramcontent.com/pod-product-compliance
Lightning Source LLC
LaVergne TN
LVHW051335050326
832903LV00031B/3549